MAYA CULTURE & COSTUME

A Catalogue of the Taylor Museum's E. B. Ricketson Collection of Guatemalan Textiles

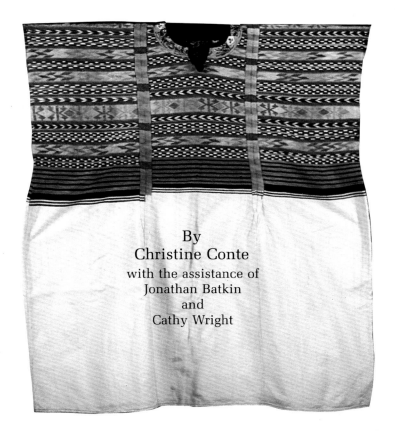

By
Christine Conte
with the assistance of
Jonathan Batkin
and
Cathy Wright

The Taylor Museum
of the
Colorado Springs Fine Arts Center
1984

LIBRARY OF CONGRESS CATALOGING IN PUBLICATION DATA

Conte, Christine, 1952-
Maya culture and costume.

Bibliography: p. 116
Includes index.

1. Mayas—Textile industry and fabrics—Catalogs. 2. Mayas—Costume and adornment—Catalogs. 3. Indians of Central America—Guatemala—Textile industry and fabrics—Catalogs. 4. Indians of Central America—Guatemala—Costume and adornment—Catalogs. 5. Ricketson, Edith Bayles, 1899-1976—Ethnological collections—Catalogs. 6. Taylor Museum—Catalogs. I. Taylor Museum. II. Title.
F1465.3.T4C66 1984   746.9'2'097281074018856   84-40115

ISBN 0-916537-00-5

PHOTOGRAPHIC CREDITS

Figures 27, 38, 40, 57, 73,
 84, 107, 136, 137, 140, 147   W. L. Bowers
Figure 9   Lowie Museum of Anthropology, University of California, Berkeley
Figure 31   The University Museum of the University of Pennsylvania, Philadelphia
Cover and color plates on pages 22, 23, 24   Gordon W. Frost, Newhall, California
All others by author

CREDITS

Editor: Jonathan Batkin
Design: Christina Watkins
Art Production: Håkan Carheden
Type: Eurostile Extended with Melior text
Typesetting and Composition: Mel Typesetting, Denver, Colorado
Color Separations: Visi Color, Inc., Denver, Colorado
Printing: Williams Printing, Inc., Colorado Springs, Colorado
Text Paper: Warren Cameo dull book and Mohawk superfine book
Cover Paper: Warren Cameo dull cover
Edition: 3000 softbound

PHOTOGRAPHS REPRODUCED COURTESY OF:

Figures 24, 55, 78, 112, 119, 125, 135:
 Historic Costume and Textile Study Collection, Department of Clothing
 and Textiles, Faculty of Home Economics, University of Alberta,
 Edmonton, Alberta, Canada T6G 2M8 (Alberta).

Figures 12, 65, 98, 109, 143:
 Library Services Department, American Museum of Natural History (AMNH).

Figures 10, 16, 17, 20, 23, 26, 28, 29, 45, 59, 75, 76, 79, 99, 115, 123,
 126, 134, 139:
 Gordon W. Frost, Newhall, California (Gordon Frost Collection).

Figures 34, 42, 86, 96, 117:
 The Heard Museum, Phoenix, Arizona (Heard).

Figures 9, 22, 37, 39, 58, 129, 144:
 Lowie Museum of Anthropology, University of California, Berkeley (Lowie).

Figures 18, 41, 51, 81, 90, 92, 93, 103:
 Middle American Research Institute, Tulane University, New Orleans (MARI).

Figures 11, 31, 35, 67, 69, 100, 121, 222, 127, 133:
 The University Museum, University of Pennsylvania (Penn).

Figures 49, 61, 64, 71, 82, 87, 94, 138, 145:
 Museum of Cultural History, University of California, Los Angeles (UCLA).

(Abbreviations used in captions; TM: The Taylor Museum.)

CONTENTS

Guatemala
1. San Pedro Ayampuc, **2.** Mixco, **3.** San Pedro Sacatepéquez, **4.** San Juan Sacatepéquez, **5.** San Pedro Churrancho.
Sacatepequez
6. Sumpango, **7.** Santo Domingo Xenacoj, **8.** Santa María Cauque, **9.** Magdalena Milpas Altas, **10.** San Antonio Aguas Calientes.
Chimaltenango
11. San José Poaquil, **12.** San Martín Jilotepeque, **13.** San Juan Comalapa, **14.** Santa Apolonia, **15.** Tecpán, **16.** Acatenango and San Antonio Nejapa, **17.** San Andres Itzapa, **18.** Santa Cruz Balanyá.
Escuintla
19. Palín
Sololá
20. Sololá, **21.** Santa Lucía Utatlán, **22.** Santa Catarina Nahualá, **23.** San Andrés Semetabaj, **24.** Panajachel, **25.** Santa Cruz la Laguna, **26.** San Marcos la Laguna, **27.** San Lucas Tólimán, **28.** Santiago Atitlán.
Totonicapán
29. Totonicapán, **30.** Santa María Chiquimula, **31.** Momostenango, **32.** San Cristóbal Totonicapán.
Quezaltenango
33. Quezaltenango, **34.** Olintepeque, **35.** San Juan Ostuncalco, **36.** Cancepción Chiquirichapa, **37.** San Martín Sacatepéquez (Chile Verde), **38.** Almolonga, **39.** Zunil.
San Marcos
40. San Marcos, **41.** San Pedro Sacatepéquez.
Huehuetenango
42. Aguacatán, **43.** Chiantla, **44.** Santa Eulalia, **45.** San Mateo Ixtatán, **46.** San Miguel Acatán, **47.** Jacaltenango, **48.** San Pedro Necta, **49.** Santiago Chimaltenango, **50.** San Rafael Petzal, **51.** Todos Santos Cuchumatán, **52.** Huehuetenango.
El Quiché
53. Santa Cruz del Quiché, **54.** Chiché, **55.** Joyabaj and Zacualpa, **56.** Santo Tomás Chichicastenango, **57.** San Juan Cotzal, **58.** Sacapulas.
Baja Verpaz
59. San Miguel Chicaj and San Gabriel Pansuj, **60.** Rabinal.

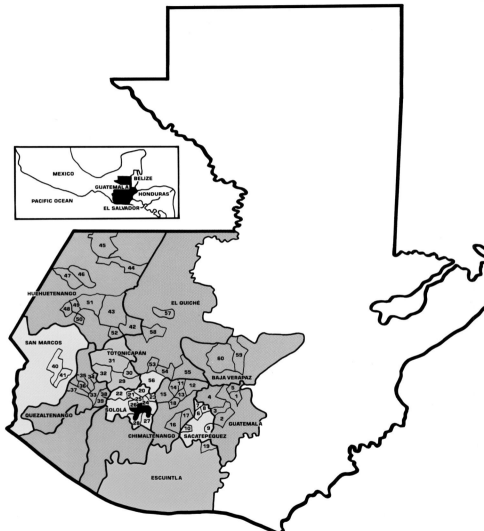

Acknowledgments

The research for and publication of this catalogue would not have been possible without the assistance and kind cooperation of numerous individuals and institutions. First mention must go to the National Endowment for the Arts for the financial support that brought this project to fruition.

The following institutions and their staff members, although not responsible for what is written here, deserve special mention: the Middle American Research Institute, Tulane University, E. Wyllys Andrews V; The University of Alberta, Edmonton, Anne M. Lambert and Elizabeth Richards; the Lowie Museum of Anthropology, University of California at Berkeley, Frank A. Norick; the Heard Museum, Erin Younger and Diana Pardue; Museum of Cultural History, University of California at Los Angeles, Patricia Altman and Patricia Anawalt; the University Museum of the University of Pennsylvania, Claudia Medoff; the American Museum of Natural History; the Peabody Museum of Archaeology and Ethnology, Harvard University, Sally Bond. I am also grateful to Gordon Frost and his family for their warm hospitality while I studied his collection.

Thanks are given to the entire staff of the Colorado Springs Fine Arts Center for the interest, expertise, and time they devoted to this project during and following my tenure as assistant curator there. Special mention is due to Arne Hansen, former director of the Fine Arts Center, under whom it was initiated, and Paul Piazza, director of the Fine Arts Center, under whom it was completed; Dr. William Wroth, former curator and Jonathan Batkin, curator of the Fine Arts Center's Taylor Museum, who carefully edited the manuscript and prepared it for publication; Christina Kreps and Cathy Wright, curatorial assistants; T. Roderick Dew, librarian; Josie Kerstetter, administrative assistant, and Kelly Smith and Emma Lerma-Sitarski, curatorial secretaries.

Several individuals have offered valuable criticisms and suggestions on the manuscript. Hilda Pang, associate professor of anthropology at Indiana State University, graciously contributed her expertise in the field as consultant and manuscript reader, as did Patricia Anawalt, consulting curator of textiles, Museum of Cultural History, University of California at Los Angeles. Gordon Frost, noted lecturer, field guide, and collector offered valuable criticism. Laura Brousseau of Westview Press, Boulder, Colorado, provided many important ideas on content and presentation of the manuscript. Mrs. William R. Bullard, Jr. (daughter of E. B. Ricketson) offered background on Mrs. Ricketson's career and provided photographs of her mother.

Finally, this catalogue is respectfully dedicated to the Maya weavers of Highland Guatemala.

Edith Bayles Ricketson at Uaxactún, Guatemala (or possibly Quiriguá, Guatemala), ca. 1928 or 1930.

INTRODUCTION

WHEN THE CATALOGUE of the Taylor Museum's Edith Bayles Ricketson collection of Guatemalan textiles was first conceived, the goal was simply to document this exceptionally fine, previously unpublished collection, assembled by Ricketson (1899-1976), an archaeologist and ethnographer. In the late 1920s and the 1930s, she lived in Guatemala where, along with her husband Oliver G. Ricketson, she worked as an archaeologist on projects sponsored by the Carnegie Institution. During this period she systematically collected Indian textiles representative of the different villages of Highland Guatemala. Collections were assembled by Mrs. Ricketson for the Museum of the American Indian, Heye Foundation in New York, and for the Peabody Museum of Archaeology and Ethnology at Harvard University. A third was sold in 1941 to the Taylor Museum of the Colorado Springs Fine Arts Center.

The Taylor Museum collection consists of more than 300 individual textiles representing seventy villages of Highland Guatemala. A large group of complete men's and women's costumes of all the major styles is included, as well as a group of less well known substyles from each of the villages represented. Garments and some complete costumes from remote villages, which have not been documented in the literature, are also found in this remarkably comprehensive collection.

As research proceeded on the catalogue, and costume descriptions from the literature were compared to the textiles in the Taylor Museum collection, it became apparent that the literature tends to minimize the degree of stylistic variability within a village or regional costume style. Questions then arose concerning the range and meaning of these variants as well as the manner in which the Ricketson collection would compare to collections of earlier and later textiles. Such comparisons are limited, however, by the fact that only seven of approximately forty major museum and private collections in North America have been published and made readily accessible to the researcher.

Dating from the 1900s to the late 1970s, these collections represent a more complete record of Maya textile history than can be observed in Highland Guatemala today, given that most garments (except those made expressly for special occasions) are worn more or less continuously and consequently do not last more than a few years. With this in mind, nine of the most comprehensive collections were selected for study and comparison with that of the Taylor Museum. The primary resource for locating and selecting the collections to be studied was the list of major museum and private collections of Guatemalan textiles compiled by Dr. Hilda Pang of Indiana State University. Within these collections, only garments from villages represented in the Taylor Museum were studied. The collections are as follows:

Institution or Private Collector	Original Collector	Dates of Collection	Approximate Number of Items
University of Alberta, Edmonton	Anne Lambert	1975	1,000
The American Museum of Natural History, New York	Rev. H. Th. Heyde Emil Mosongi Herbert J. Spinden	1901 1907 1917	600
Gordon W. Frost, Newhall, California	Gordon W. Frost	1965-1975	5,000
The Heard Museum, Phoenix	James F. Bell	1970-1971	200
Lowie Museum of Anthropology, University of California, Berkeley	Gustav Eisen	1901	500
Middle American Research Institute, Tulane University, New Orleans	Mathilda Geddings Gray	1930s	200
Museum of Cultural History, University of California, Los Angeles	Caroline and Howard West	1970s	300
Peabody Museum of Archaeology and Ethnology, Harvard University, Cambridge	Howard H. Tewkesbury Edith B. Ricketson Ruth Reeves Mr. and Mrs. Clyde Williams Dr. S. K. Lothrop	1930s 1932 1934 1933 1930s	500
The University Museum of the University of Pennsylvania, Philadelphia	Lilly de Jongh Osborne Robert Burkett Howard H. Tewkesbury Ruben Reina	1930s and 1940s 1910-1920 1936-1940 1969-1970	600
The Taylor Museum of the Colorado Springs Fine Arts Center	Edith B. Ricketson	1932-1934	300

Through the comparative study and documentation of these collections, the scope of the catalogue expanded to include an encyclopedic overview and chronology of village styles of Guatemalan textiles. The range and content of stylistic variability in Guatemalan Indian costume from Precolumbian times to the present are explored together with the cultural and historical background needed to explain stylistic change and persistence in the Maya weaver's art. It is hoped that this preliminary study will provide data to which similar Guatemalan textile collections can be compared and that the stylistic trends identified in the present study can be verified. Most importantly, once questions have been answered regarding the amount and type of stylistic variability existing through time and space in Guatemalan textiles, attention can be turned to the more difficult and interesting problems of the cultural and societal meanings of the Maya weaver's art in historical perspective: How has weaving changed in response to and in turn influenced the structure and dynamics of Maya culture and society in Highland Guatemala? This catalogue seeks to organize and make accessible some of the rich resources of twentieth-century Guatemalan textile collections. It also aims to further research in the field by calling attention to the potential of collections not yet studied.

Following in a tradition that is centuries old, the Highland Maya have become justly famous for the skill, beauty, and variety of their weaving. The most significant products of the Maya loom are a dazzling array of costumes, which, among other things, identify the wearer's village or regional affiliation. In the mid-1960s, approximately 200 recognizably different costume styles could be identified in Guatemala, a country no larger than the state of New York. If substyles within the villages were to be included, the number of distinct styles would soar to approximately 500 (Osborne 1965:9).

Guatemalan textiles, which until very recently have been made solely for use by the native population rather than for commercial export, can be appreciated not only for their purely aesthetic qualities, but also as physical expressions of Maya culture. As such, they are rich in symbolic content. The creative manipulation of symbols is a universal and uniquely human process. Symbols pervade all social relationships from the mundane economics of daily subsistence to the esoteric panoply of sacred ritual. Communication is their purpose. The means of communication are diverse and may involve behavior, language, or visual arts. Symbols organize disparate social elements in order to satisfy utilitarian needs (to get things done) and to create a congruence of spiritual, expressive, or aesthetic values. They may be used singly or combined in specified ways. The patterned combination of symbols in material culture is recognized both intuitively and analytically in the identification of styles.

The use of symbols or styles enables people to define boundaries between their own group and those of others. In traditional societies material culture (pottery, basketry, farming tools, or textiles, for example) embodies information about the people that produce it — about their culture and history; their view of the world and their place in it; the manner in which they distinguish themselves from, or ally themselves with, outsiders; and the way that they relate to others in their own society. In this manner Guatemalan textiles, and especially the variety of their styles and substyles in costume garments, serve not only obvious utilitarian functions, but also mark ethnic or community affiliation, social status, religious belief, aesthetic value, occupation, age, sex, and individual identity. As a society responds both to internal changes and foreign influences, material culture will reflect in varying degrees these changes and influences. Nowhere is this more true than in Highland Guatemala, where archaeological, historical, and ethnographic sources reveal a history of repeated contacts among internal populations and with foreigners. Guatemalan textiles reflect the impact of these contacts and constitute a rich account of a living culture.

Men praying on the steps of the
church at Santo Tomás
Chichicastenango, El Quiché, early
twentieth century. Taylor Museum
photo archives.

MAYA WEAVING
Culture History and Textile Development

THE GEOGRAPHICAL SETTING. The Guatemalan Highlands constitute a distinct geographical unit containing, and to a large extent, determining social interaction within its boundaries. Over 70 percent of Guatemala's 2.5 million Maya Indians, divided into fourteen related Maya language groups, live in the Highlands, and the majority are concentrated in the western and central regions. The Indian population is predominantly rural in contrast to the city- or town-dwelling *Ladinos* (people of mixed Spanish and Indian blood, or those who have adopted western culture). An extensive and rugged region with elevations ranging from 4,000 to over 10,000 feet above sea level and a generally temperate climate, the Highlands constitute an extension of the Andean cordillera.

On the northwest border rise the jagged peaks of the Cuchumatanes mountains. Home of the Mam-, Kanjobal-, Ixil-, Jacaltec-, and Aguacatec-speaking Maya peoples, the northwestern Highlands are characterized by extremes of altitude and climate: within a few miles of each other are cold, mist-shrouded mountain passes and lush, semi-tropical valleys. Steep volcanoes separate the western border of the Highland plateau from an escarpment that rapidly descends to the Pacific coast.

The midwestern Highlands are intersected by hills and steep-sided canyons, called *barrancas,* which greatly increase the isolation of local communities. The vast majority of the midwestern Highland population is Maya. Quiché, Cakchiquel, and Tzutujil are the largest language groups; Rabinal and Uspantec speakers constitute smaller groups. At the center of the area is magnificent Lake Atitlán surrounded by steep cliffs, verdant mountains, and majestic volcanoes.

Only on the eastern slope of the Highland plateau, including the departments of Guatemala, Alta Verapaz, Baja Verapaz, Jalapa, Escuintla, and El Progreso, is the terrain less broken, with low, rolling mountains and hills and streams running to the Atlantic coast. Unlike the populations of the other two regions, that of the eastern Highlands is predominantly *Ladino*. Because of extensive Western contact and settlement, the native way of life, including the aspect of native costume, has been considerably modified. However, in communities where the native Maya languages of Pokomam, Kekchi, Chorti, and Pokomchi have not been supplanted by Spanish, native textile arts have been preserved, largely by the village women.

THE PRECOLUMBIAN PERIOD. The culture history of the Maya of Highland Guatemala is intimately linked with that of their Maya neighbors of Lowland Guatemala, Belize, and the Yucatan peninsula of Mexico, as well as with various non-Maya peoples of Mexico. Centuries of intensive trade, population migrations, and intermittent violent contact between these Highland and Lowland groups are responsible for the fairly uniform repertory of Precolumbian Mesoamerican garment types, as well as for the interregional similarities that remain today in the Guatemalan Highlands.

The florescence of Maya civilization in Guatemala took place during the Classic period (300-900 A.D.), not on the Highland plateau but in the jungle lowlands of the Petén. Monumental political and ceremonial centers such as Tikal and Uaxactún arose in this hot and humid environment. These impressive centers, with pyramids, temples, palaces, and great low-relief stone sculptures called stelae, were inhabited by the upper echelon of the social hierarchy: nobility, religious, military, and in some cases, occupational specialists such as musicians, nursemaids, and various types of artisans. Achievements in the arts and sciences were accomplished here, conferring upon the area the privileged title of "civilization." The Maya calendrical system, based upon a sophisticated understanding of astronomy and mathematics, is preserved and used in the Highlands today. Calendrical, astronomical, and astrological implications of the Maya hieroglyphic writing system were partially deciphered by the turn of the century. Only recently have studies begun to yield information on the successive reigns of Maya political leaders.

By 900 A.D., perhaps due to military onslaughts by Mexican invaders and internal social disruptions, Maya civilization of the Petén Lowlands had collapsed. The political and ceremonial centers were rather abruptly abandoned, populations were dispersed, and the socially stratified theocracy was destroyed. During the ensuing Postclassic period (900-1524 A.D.), there occurred a devastation of the social order and disunity of Lowland society. By the time of the Spanish conquest in the sixteenth century, this was evident in the defacement of artworks and the grafitti scrawled on the walls of the sacred temples. Due to the inability of the remaining population to defend itself, the Spaniards soon controlled the area and imposed a new social, cultural, and technological order. Contemporary Maya art and culture of Lowland Guatemala bear little resemblance to that of their preconquest past.

Because of the dearth of archaeological excavations in the Highlands, far less information is available about the Precolumbian period there. The earliest known settlements in Guatemala were on the Pacific coast and date as far back as the Early Preclassic period (1500-800 B.C.). Archaeological records indicate that a population shift took place from the Pacific coast to the Highlands in the Late Preclassic period (300 B.C.-300 A.D.).

Much of our information about the Classic period in Guatemala (300-900 A.D.) comes from the site of Kaminaljuyú in the midwestern Highland valley where the modern capital of Guatemala City is located. With a population estimated at 25,000 by 600 B.C., Kaminaljuyú boasted a great number of rectangular adobe platform mounds as high as 65.6 feet and tomb burials with lavish offerings suggesting a stratified society ruled by ranked lineages (Sanders 1969:164-165). Sculptural styles, hieroglyphs, ceramic trade vessels, and stelae (indicating elite group literacy at least) provide evidence of widespread trade and subsequent influence from other areas of Mesoamerica. Shells from the Pacific coast and jade from central Mexico have also been found (Thompson 1964).

By 600 A.D. when northern Lowland society was at its cultural peak, Highland culture seems to have come under the direct hegemony of the great and powerful city of Teotihuacán, near what is now Mexico City. Features in architecture and ceramics, as well as in the patterns of population settlement, suggest that sociopolitical power at Kaminaljuyú was actually vested in foreign rulers from Teotihuacán. Furthermore, some midwestern Highland sites were replaced by new sites in the northwestern and eastern Highlands, positioned so as to facilitate trade with the Petén Lowlands. These new sites were strategically located in a long-distance trade network dominated by Teotihuacán until its collapse around 600 A.D., and the subsequent decline and abandonment of Kaminaljuyú. There are indications that a contemporary resurgence of native Highland Maya culture and a redirection of trade networks to an intraregional orientation took place following the collapse.

During the Postclassic period (900-1524 A.D.) in Highland Guatemala, competitive political systems arose roughly corresponding to present-day ethnic and linguistic boundaries (for example the Cakchiquel-Tzutujil area around Lake Atitlán vs. the Quiché-Maya region in the adjacent highlands). This phenomenon is associated with the influx of Classic Lowland Maya and various Mexican cultural forms that began to occur in many Highland sites in the Late Classic period (600-900 A.D.). However, in the central Quiché area (surrounding the present-day town of Santa Cruz del Quiché), regional provincialism was not disrupted until around 1250 A.D., when there occurred an intrusion of small bands of warriors from the Tabasco-Veracruz area of the Mexican Gulf coast. The conquerors, of Toltec ancestry from the collapsed elite center of Tula in central Mexico, spoke both the Nahuatl language of their forefathers and the Chontal Maya of the Gulf coast.

Although they adoped the native Quiché language and the name Quiché, these Gulf coast invaders imposed many changes on native culture that are apparent in archaeological, documentary, and linguistic records. Evidence of these changes includes new architectural forms and settlement patterns, the introduction of Nahuatl words into the Quiché language, Mexican religious symbolism, the practice of human sacrifice to appease cosmological deities, and a complex sociopolitical organization based upon hereditary aristocracy and empire building through conquest. By the late fifteenth century the Quiché empire and sphere of influence included most of the Guatemalan Highlands and extended as far north as the state of Chiapas, Mexico. It is probable that internecine warfare in the decades prior to the Spanish conquest had so weakened the Quiché empire that it would have been easy prey for the encroaching Aztecs of central Mexico had the Spaniards not arrived first (Carmack 1981).

DEVELOPMENT OF THE WEAVER'S ART. The development of weaving technology and costume styles in Precolumbian Guatemala can be inferred from the archaeological record. Because only a few fragments of actual fabric have survived, the story must be pieced together using a variety of indirect sources, not only from Highland Guatemala, but also from areas of Mexico and Guatemala thought to have been in contact with, or to have otherwise influenced, the Highlands. Evidence of textile technology and design comes from fabric impressions on pottery and dried mud, from clay figurines, and from clothed figures depicted on painted ceramic vessels, stelae, stone relief carvings, frescoes, murals, and codices.

Weaving was probably established firmly in Highland Guatemala, as in most other areas of Mesoamerica, by 1500 B.C. For example, similarities between garment types represented on figurines from Ecuador as early as 1500 B.C. and those portrayed in the archaeological record of West Mexico (500 B.C.-500 A.D.) suggest contact between the two areas some millennia before the Spanish conquest (Anawalt 1981: personal communication). Clay whorls from spindles used to spin cotton have been excavated at Kaminaljuyú and at other Highland Guatemalan sites dated as early as 300 A.D. Although Maya legend credits Hunahpú, eighth king of the Quiché, with the introduction of cotton to Guatemala (Osborne 1965:22), the archaeological record indicates that at least two varieties have been cultivated since about 1500 B.C. (Coe 1977:47). Anawalt believes that the weaving of cotton was probably the prerogative of the upper classes only and that the lower classes probably wore clothing woven from a variety of bast fibers such as those of the maguey plant (Anawalt 1981: personal communication). These are still spun and used today for hammocks, net bags, and some types of sash.

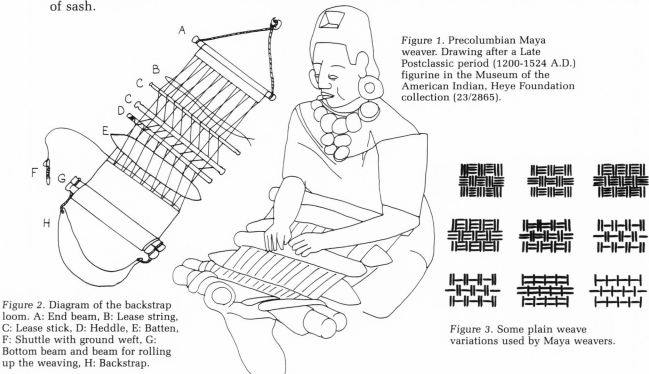

Figure 1. Precolumbian Maya weaver. Drawing after a Late Postclassic period (1200-1524 A.D.) figurine in the Museum of the American Indian, Heye Foundation collection (23/2865).

Figure 2. Diagram of the backstrap loom. A: End beam, B: Lease string, C: Lease stick, D: Heddle, E: Batten, F: Shuttle with ground weft, G: Bottom beam and beam for rolling up the weaving, H: Backstrap.

Figure 3. Some plain weave variations used by Maya weavers.

Silky native vegetal fibers and filaments produced by various caterpillars and spiders may have been incorporated into prehistoric Guatemalan weaving, but thus far evidence of their use comes only from other areas of Central America. Cloth imprints on dried mud and fired clay have been found at numerous Lowland Maya sites, at the Highland Guatemalan sites of Kaminaljuyú, Zaculeu, Utatlán, and Nebaj, and at several smaller Highland sites in the present-day departments of Suchitepéquez and Baja Verapaz. The simple over-one-under-one technique known as plain weave predominates in these specimens, but the more elaborate gauze, canvas, and lace weaves also appear. Basic tools of the contemporary Maya weaver — a spindle whorl, warping stakes, and backstrap loom — have remained virtually unchanged since Precolumbian times.

With the exception of warriors' costumes, clothing throughout Mesoamerica was characteristically worn loosely draped rather than cut or tailored to follow the contours of the body (Anawalt 1977:108). The principal garments worn by men were a loincloth, hip cloth or kilt, and a cape. Women wore a *huipil* (a loose-fitting, sleeveless, upper garment), or a *quechquemitl* (a short poncho with pointed front and back), together with a wraparound skirt and a hair tie. These garments were constructed of square or rectangular pieces of fabric and required either a single length of cloth, or two or more pieces sewn together. Fringes or other decorations may have been added to them. The modern-day Maya man's costume bears little resemblance to its prehistoric counterpart. However, the contemporary woman's costume, specifically the wraparound skirt or *corte*, the *huipil*, and some types of headdress, is descended directly from the prehistoric forms.

The clothing of the prehistoric Maya clearly reflects the highly stratified nature of their social order. Costumes of the deities and the upper classes, as depicted in surviving illustrations, appear so ornate and bedecked with fringes, precious stones, metals, and feathers that it is difficult to distinguish the cut of the underlying garment, much less to glean information about the weaving techniques employed. Men of the noble classes wore all of the basic garments described above (with the addition of flamboyant headdresses and sashes), while those of the lowest class wore no more than a plain cotton loincloth. Garments of both upper-class men and women also incorporated brilliantly colored design motifs of geometric forms, animals, and plants. These designs were either embroidered onto the fabric after weaving or were woven into the fabric itself — a technique called supplementary weft patterning, commonly referred to as brocade. Some of these prehistoric design motifs appear to have direct correspondence to textile motifs still used by the modern-day Maya of Highland Guatemala (Pang 1977b:393-394).

The fresco murals from the Lowland site of Bonampak (Figure 4) provide what are perhaps the best illustrations of ancient Maya costumes. These colorful murals portray slaves, servants, commoners, members of the nobility, warriors, and such occupational specialists as artisans and musicians, all engaged in a variety of ceremonial and daily activities. Each social category is distinguishable by activity and costume design.

The costumes depicted on the Bonampak murals, along with those found on murals and relief sculptures from other Lowland Maya sites, such as Uaxactún, have provided important information about the structure and dynamics of ancient Maya society. For example, most of the individual figures portrayed in Maya art appear to be male, indicating a patriarchal social organization. However, one Maya archaeologist and art historian, Tatiana Proskouriakoff (1961), was able to demonstrate through a careful study of costume, gesture, and stance, particularly with regard to the posture and relationship of figures, that some individuals assumed to be male were actually female. Furthermore, she observed that during the Lowland Maya Late Classic period (600-900 A.D.), female figures began to play a more prominent role in Maya art and in many cases, including the Bonampak murals, they were depicted in positions denoting equal status with male figures. Women were occasionally even represented

Figure 4. "The Arraignment of Prisoners." Detail of the mural from Room 2 at the Lowland Maya site of Bonampak. Men and women of the nobility are depicted in elaborate costumes along with scantily clad retainers and prisoners.

as participants in bloodletting ceremonies and in the assignment of prisoners. This suggested to Proskouriakoff that during the Late Classic period, women of the noble class assumed positions of leadership in religious and political activities previously monopolized by men. In the Yaxchilán reliefs, from the Lowland site of Uaxactún, female commoners are identified by the relative simplicity of their costume and their association with children in the capacity of nurse-servants. The presence of such figures, in conjunction with other types of archaeological evidence from this site, led Proskouriakoff to question the commonly held assumption that most Lowland Maya art was religious, and to postulate a Late Classical trend towards secularization.

In general, the archaeological record of textile technology and costume design in the highlands of Guatemala is far too sketchy to permit detailed research on the interrelationships between textile arts and society. However, there is evidence that elaborate costumes were worn by some classes of native Guatemalans even prior to the rise of the Quiché empire in the Late Postclassic period (1200-1524 A.D.). For example, several stelae from Kaminaljuyú portray warriors with complex plumed headdresses and decorated kilts and sashes. Later, around 1250 A.D., the Gulf coast Mexican invaders were most impressed with the ornate costumes of their Quiché adversaries, which included crowns and lances adorned with metal (Carmack 1981:60).

Recent excavations at Utatlán, the Late Postclassic capital of the Quiché empire, have yielded a mural depicting a warrior in full regalia performing a ritual dance of Toltec origin (Figure 5, page 29). Many features of the dancer's costume also reflect the Toltec heritage of the Quiché nobility. These include the shield of twisted vines or string, the gourd tobacco pouch pendant, and a pair of wristbands with a Nahuatl-derived name. Garments whose ethnic origins are yet to be identified are sandals, feathered leg bands, a decorated loincloth over the top of a short kilt, and what appears to be a tasseled pouch or sash hanging from the dancer's waist. Unfortunately, the mural is too schematically drawn to allow a very detailed analysis of the textiles represented there, but some features may be noted and compared. Around the dancer's neck is a solar disk associated with Tojil, the Quiché sky and war god (Carmack 1981:297-299). The disk is similar to the appliquéd neckline design on twentieth-century women's *huipiles* of several municipalities (cf. p. 48, Figure 54; p. 81, Figure 132) and men's jackets from Chichicastenango (p. 54, Figure 56).

So little data on Precolumbian costumes are available from other areas of the Guatemalan Highlands as to preclude stylistic interpretation. Many questions remain concerning the nature of foreign and internal relationships and the way in which these relationships affected the development of regional costume styles in Highland Guatemala. Perhaps future excavations at Utatlán and other Highland sites will provide some answers. For example, representations of the elaborately decorated textiles of the nobility would most likely include symbols of ancestry and social rank — important clues for unraveling the little understood cultural history of the Maya Highlands before the Spanish conquest.

THE SPANISH CONQUEST. Pedro de Alvarado, with a force of less than 300 Spaniards and approximately 200 Tlaxcalan and Cholulan Mexican Indians, accomplished the conquest of Guatemala, whose native forces have been estimated at around 30,000 warriors, in less than a year (late 1523-July 1524). The Spaniards, with the help of their native allies, conquered the native populations and set up their first capital in the middle of a cornfield near Iximché, former capital of the Cakchiquel people. The swiftness with which the conquest was accomplished can be attributed to several factors. The superiority of Spanish firearms against the obsidian-tipped spears, and the psychological advantage these powerful weapons imparted to the conquistadors, were primary factors. It was also significant that the natives attributed fearful supernatural powers to the strange white men astride four-legged beasts. Finally, Alvarado was able to enlist the aid of native allies by playing effectively upon the long-standing and bitter rivalries among the various Highland kingdoms of the time (Jones 1940:7). Anawalt believes that another factor facilitating the conquest was the decimation of a large proportion of the Highland population by such Old World diseases as smallpox (Anawalt 1981: personal communication). These diseases had already spread into the Highlands from Mexico before Alvarado's onslaught.

In succeeding decades the Spaniards were to subjugate further and reorganize drastically the native Guatemalan society, creating a disjuncture of great magnitude with the Precolumbian past. During the early conquest period, the major changes in Highland Maya life centered on the consolidation of dispersed rural settlements, the attempted conversion of the population to Catholicism, and the termination of intertribal warfare. This was accomplished by removing the highest level of native leadership and replacing it with Spanish officials.

Despite these changes, however, Maya society of the Guatemalan Highlands was never so thoroughly disrupted as that of the Lowlands. Instead, the impact of the conquest caused the transformation rather than the total destruction of native Highland society. The indigenous way of life — social, economic, political, and cultural — was molded but not eradicated by the conquerors through the selective imposition of Spanish institutions deemed most applicable to the New World (Foster 1960:14). The continuity of Highland Maya life was encouraged by the rugged and diverse character of the Highland landscape, making some areas unreachable and/or inhospitable to Spanish farming techniques or other enterprises. Different degrees and types of contact also contributed to an increase in the heterogeneity of Maya culture and effected the development of new systems of communication and exchange among the various subgroups (Nash 1969:41). Finally, concepts of racial and cultural purity on the part of both Spaniards and natives, bolstered by material differences, helped to preserve a significant degree of Maya self-sufficiency and indigenous culture.

The colonial economy was based on the control of Indian labor. Extraction of surplus agricultural products and other resources was effected, while the Indians were forced to maintain their own subsistence. Two systems of labor control, transplanted from the Old World to Highland Guatemala, supported this economic system: *encomienda* and *repartimiento*. *Encomienda* was made possible by the granting of large tracts of land and the labor of Indians living on them to loyal colonists who assumed the obligation to enforce Christianity among the Indians. *Repartimiento* was the resettlement or relocation of native peoples for the purpose of creating native work groups controlled by an Indian foreman.

Neither of these methods to secure Indian labor power would have been successful if the Spaniards had not reorganized the native pattern of settlement, consolidating as many as twenty scattered rural villages into one town or *municipio*. Laid out in the Old World grid pattern with a central plaza and Catholic church and with agricultural fields surrounding the town, *municipios* were sometimes located on or near the sites of preconquest ceremonial centers. The new settlement pattern, which made more Indian land available for Spanish colonists, facilitated the collection of tribute and provided a captive audience for the proselytizing efforts of the Catholic priests.

In spite of the advantages which the Spaniards gained by their new settlement pattern, attempts to convert the Maya to orthodox Catholicism were never successful. Instead, efforts at conversion resulted in a blend of both Catholic and indigenous beliefs and practices, a folk Catholicism that is still characteristic of Highland Maya culture to this day. One prominent example of this cultural syncretism, set in motion during the colonial period and still functioning today, is the *cofradía* system. The *cofradía* (confraternity) in the Highlands is a religious hierarchy whose main purpose is to care for the images of the *municipio's* patron saint and other saints and to execute saint's day rituals. Officers, or *mayordomos*, of the *cofradía* and of the closely related civil hierarchy serve for one year without pay and often at substantial personal expense in fulfillment of community obligations. Each *mayordomo* is addressed by a term of rank, is assigned formal duties, and is given a special costume that often bears insignia of his status within the hierarchy. Special costumes are also worn by the wives of *cofradía* members when they assist their husbands in ceremonies and processions.

The highest ranking officer, the *alcalde mayor*, assumes the sacred task of caring for the image of the patron saint, which is enshrined in his household during the period of his office.

The Spanish Catholic priests originally established and sanctioned the *cofradías*, expecting to undermine the aboriginal pantheon and supplant the agricultural calendar central to Maya religion with the Christian calendar. For the Maya, however, the *cofradía* system was embraced because it was congenial to native practices and concepts. The keeping of household shrines, the decoration of statues personifying supernatural beings, the carrying of images in procession to the music of drums and flutes, and the comical antics of clowns juxtaposed with solemn ritual, are all aboriginal features transposed into the *cofradía* system. Even today many of the more traditional Maya have incorporated the Christian saints into the native pantheon and attribute to them supernatural powers not given to them by the Catholic church. For this reason, *cofradías* are now only grudgingly tolerated by the official Church, and local priests play no part in the organization.

With the abolition of *encomienda* in 1720, Spanish control was relaxed, allowing a regeneration of indigenous culture and an increase in *municipio* autonomy. Nonetheless, the conquest had long-lasting effects on all spheres of Maya life, including weaving technology and costume design.

THE COLONIAL PERIOD.
Two of the most significant colonial influences on weaving technology were the introduction of new or improved fibers and several variants of the treadle, or foot loom. At the time of the conquest both raw cotton and dyed cotton threads were abundant in native marketplaces throughout Mesoamerica. Cortés reported from central Mexico that "All kinds of cotton thread in various colors may be bought in skeins, very much in the same way as the great silk exchange in Granada. They have colors for painting of as good quality as any in Spain, and of as pure shades as may be found anywhere" (quoted in Lathbury 1974:56).

During the colonial period domestic cotton remained the basic material of backstrap weavers, but the resiliency and strength of the native varieties were improved by the introduction of a seed imported from the Far East. Also from the Far East came silk floss, an expensive and rather scarce commodity whose use, even today, is generally reserved for the decoration of ceremonial or elite-class garments. Domestic commercial production of silk was initiated in Guatemala after the conquest, but silk was never produced in sufficient quantities to displace imported floss.

By 1528, the Spaniards had brought sheep to the Guatemalan Highlands, and the spinning of wool yarn was incorporated into the technology of native weaving. The introduction of the merino sheep variety from Spain in 1630 spurred the production of wool in Guatemala, which has since become the largest producer in Central America. The thermal properties of wool were especially appreciated by peoples of the cold, high-altitude regions. However, the thick wool yarns were not as amenable to weaving on the backstrap loom as native fibers had been, and new techniques were needed to employ the new fiber to its best advantage. Two such techniques were crocheting and knitting, taught to Maya men by the Spaniards and used primarily for making men's carrying bags. Wool did not achieve much popularity in Guatemala until the seventeenth century, when the European foot or treadle loom was introduced and natives were instructed in its use. Along with the simple foot loom and the more sophisticated draw and *jacquard* variants, the Spaniards introduced the spinning wheel. These technological improvements and the Indian labor force enabled the Spanish colonists to efficiently produce fabric suitable for European-style clothing. In the village of Cubulco, Fray Domingo Carrucosa "personally instructed the Indians of that region in the style, technique, and colors preferred by the Spaniards" (Osborne 1965:55).

Indian men were set to weave on the treadle loom in workshops or factories owned by individual Spanish families while Indian women continued to make cotton cloth for their families and as tribute to the colonists. This division of labor, with men working at the foot loom and women weaving exclusively on the backstrap loom, remains substantially the same today. Men work either for others in factories or on their own looms in their households, weaving for both commercial and native markets.

While some Spanish colonial influences on the textile arts of the Highland Maya are obvious, others are subtle and difficult to isolate. In general, innovations in design are less apparent than technological innovations. There are four factors that make it difficult to pinpoint Spanish influence.

1. There was a pre-existing stylistic diversity in Maya costume (described above), with regional variations in the nature and degree of colonial influence in the Highlands.

2. Despite edicts from the Spanish crown intended to abolish native dress, such as the edict of 1563 that prohibited the use of silver or gold threads in Indian textiles (Osborne 1965:19), actual enforcement was somewhat erratic. For example, in several large Indian centers of the western Highlands, such as Quezaltenango, Utatlán, and Totonicapán, Precolumbian caste distinctions and appropriate forms of costume and design motifs were left intact (Osborne 1965:148, Lathbury 1974:17). In other *municipios* (Chichicastenango, Ciudad Vieja, and Mixco among them), the traditional status hierarchy and undoubtedly the wearing of traditional costume were disrupted by the crown's appointment of Tlaxcalan Indian mercenaries to positions of power as a reward for their role in the conquest (Lathbury 1974:17-18).

3. An additional complicating factor in deciphering Spanish colonial influences on Maya textile designs stems from the fact that the conquerors represented different cultural areas of Spain, each area having particular customs and styles of dress. These groups tended to colonize specific geographical regions of Guatemala, adding further to the regionalization of Highland culture and costume.

4. In colonial times Guatemala was subdivided into religious districts, each placed under the control of a specific religious order. Each order had a distinct philosophy and congruent program for Christianizing, governing, and "civilizing" its wards (Delgado 1963:393).

Along with technological and economic changes, some striking innovations in Maya costume style during the colonial period have also been documented. Modifications in the cut of garments and in the style of wearing particular garments and variations in design motifs appear at this time. With the exception of Precolumbian warriors' garb, the concept of tailored clothing, most notably as applied to men's shirts and woolen jackets, was a Spanish introduction. Osborne has suggested, for example, that the *capixay*, a dark wool tunic worn by men, may have been inspired by the habits of sixteenth century monks (Osborne 1965:20). The

Milpas (corn fields) just outside of the town of Santa Cruz del Quiché.

Lake Atitlán at the center of the midwestern Highlands, is surrounded by steep cliffs, verdant mountains, and majestic volcanoes.

Woman and child from San Ildefonso Ixtahuacán, Huehuetenango.
© Gordon Frost.

Woman from Chichicastenango, El Quiché, weaving on backstrap loom.

Men from Todos Santos Cuchumatán,
Huehuetenango. © Gordon Frost.

Woman weaver from San Gabriel
Pansuj, Baja Verapaz. © Gordon Frost.

women's custom of covering the head with a veil, folded head cloth, or *huipil,* as an expression of religious humility, also stems from colonial religious influence.

Three types of Spanish clothing which influenced Highland Maya costume, and the approximate dates of their introduction to the area, are distinguished in Anawalt's careful study (1977:109). The historical prototype of the treadle-loomed jacket and trousers worn by men in the *municipio* of Chichicastenango is a man's suit fashionable in nineteenth-century Andalusia in southern Spain. Parallels can be drawn between the Quezaltenango woman's pleated skirt, tucked-in *huipil,* and sashed waist and the nineteenth-century southern Spanish woman's costume. The man's costume of San Juan Sacatepéquez, with the notched and braid-trimmed lapel of its jacket, semifitted trousers, and brightly sashed waist is derivative of yet another man's costume of nineteenth-century southern Spain.

Design motifs that appear on contemporary Highland Maya garments are known to have existed in the Old World before the Spanish conquest and could have been introduced into the Highlands as early as the mid-sixteenth century. Furthermore, even at this early date, there was a highly active interchange of design styles in central Europe and some of the motifs introduced into the New World by the Spanish may have originated in Italy, Germany, or France. For example, Pang notes that "Preceding the Contact period, there existed in Spain at the folk level, a tradition of small, free form, simplified animal, plant and human motifs often combined into bands, which could have influenced the design of Mesoamerican colonial period textiles" (Pang 1977b:389).

The elaborately decorated church vestments and altar cloths, particularly those found in the larger *municipios* where the Spanish clergy was most firmly established, display the richest European influence on Guatemalan design. Those textiles may have been vehicles for introducing new motifs into the Indian repertory. Documents that support this hypothesis reveal that priests and nuns in Mexico and Guatemala instructed the Indians in the art of embroidery using pattern books brought from the Old World.

The incidence of the double-headed bird motif is a well-documented case of direct introduction of a Spanish motif into Mesoamerican weaving, and into that of Highland Guatemala in particular. Today this motif is ubiquitous in the native arts of Central America. In the sixteenth century, it was conferred by the Spanish crown upon the Nijaib Quiché as the insignia of their royal lineage, although a similar motif had been used by Maya weavers in Precolumbian times. The double-headed eagle was also the emblem of the Spanish king, Charles V. Today, textile interpretations of this symbol reflect its Spanish origin, but also include various elements of the explicitly Maya experience and belief system. For example, an Indian man from San Juan Sacatepéquez identified the bicephalous bird as a sign of noble rank in his village and as the Great God who has two faces. A woman from the same village stated that the symbol was woven into wedding *huipiles* to remind married women not to have children until the evil bird from overseas, which had so oppressed the Indian people, had been banished. In a rural hamlet of Santo Tomás Chichicastenango, an old woman offered the following explanation: The double-headed bird, named Glavicote, is now extinct, but in the beginning when Dios Mundo (Earth God) first made the earth, many such birds existed. They were very big, speckled birds that were helpful because they consumed dead animals' carcasses, but they were also much feared for their habit of swooping down and carrying off domestic animals and children. It was not until people discovered the blowgun (an aboriginal weapon rarely used in Guatemala today) that they were able to kill all the Glavicotes.

In this interpretation of the double-headed bird, the Spanish elements are overshadowed by those particular to the aboriginal Maya cosmology. As portrayed in the tale, Glavicote is most likely a counterpart of the supernatural bird, Xecotcovach, described in the legendary history of the Quiché Maya, the *Popul Vuh*. Like Glavicote, Xecotcovach roamed the new-formed earth, carried off and devoured people, and could not be killed until the mythical heroes Hunahpú and Xblanque appeared with their blowguns to shoot it down.

All of these interpretations of the double-headed bird motif clearly illustrate the complex and multiple ways in which native and Spanish colonial meanings have become intertwined, transformed, and communicated through time. Today, the origins and symbolic content of most design motifs, and there are thousands, used by Maya weavers in Highland Guatemala have been forgotten, although descriptive names are often applied to particular motifs.

The ease with which needlepoint samplers and pattern books from Europe and North America have been accepted as a source of design motifs illustrates the general lack of specific symbolic content in most motifs today. Everything from roses to teddy bears holding balloons has been prevalent in recent decades, although ceremonial textiles tend to preserve traditional motifs to a greater extent than do secular ones. Information on this phenomenon might be recovered through a combination of ethnohistorical research, study of existing textile collections, and field research on the use of various motifs in village life.

THE POSTINDEPENDENCE PERIOD.

After Guatemala gained independence from Spain in 1821, a new wave of foreign influence and pressure assaulted the Maya people. The Guatemalan central government, now consolidated in *Ladino* hands, welcomed the development of agricultural export production by foreign investors. Until the end of World War II, when U.S. corporate interests came to the forefront, the Germans dominated Guatemalan commerce. Maya lands were forcibly appropriated for German-owned coffee plantations concentrated in the fertile southwestern piedmont region of the Highlands and in the department of Alta Verapaz. The boom in foreign-controlled agricultural production, chiefly of coffee, was also responsible for the opening of roads into once isolated Indian territories. The new roads facilitated the transport not only of goods, but of Indian laborers from throughout the Highlands. These were forced to supplement their subsistence-level economic status with seasonal work for which they were paid minimal cash wages. An emphasis on nonfood export crops continues to characterize the Guatemalan national economy. This emphasis, in conjunction with the takeover of Indian lands that it necessitates and population increases, has resulted in respectable growth rates for the national economy as a whole, but has not contributed to the well-being of Guatemala's native peoples (Adams 1970). Today, 72 percent of the nation's land is owned by only 2 percent of the population and an estimated 80 percent of the children over five years of age suffer from malnutrition (Guatemala Scholars Network 1981).

Industrialization, set in motion in the nineteenth century, has also had far-reaching effects on Maya society. Centered in Guatemala City and its expanding environs, the mechanized manufacture of goods has, to some extent, undermined small-scale native production of clothing and household utensils. In some subordinate manufacturing centers such as Quezaltenango, a small class of Indians has wrested the control of industry and business from *Ladinos*. Their economic successes, however, have been achieved through affiliation with the *Ladino* ethnic group and the rejection of Maya life styles and values. Strong social and economic impediments for Maya-identified peoples constitute a major pressure toward "Ladinoization" where local prejudices permit such crossing-over. The pursuit of social status and economic success explains why so many Maya men have abandoned native costume in favor of Western clothing.

In 1876, domestic textile production was spurred by the establishment of an electric mill in the town of Cantel, Quezaltenango. Owned by a *Ladino* family and employing between 800 and 1,000 Indian workers, the mill manufactures 70 percent of all cotton thread produced in Guatemala (Nash 1967:21). At first the machine-milled thread and the cloth made from it were rejected by Indian weavers because the thread was considered too evenly spun. These products were finally accepted by the native populace when, in 1910, the factory attempted to manufacture thread with a more handspun appearance (Lathbury 1974:51). Today the vast majority of Maya weavers prefer to purchase commercial predyed thread, either foreign or domestic, rather than continue the tedious and time-consuming practice of handspinning and dyeing.

THE PRESENT.
Despite governmental centralization and the concomitant growth of nationalism in the nineteenth and twentieth centuries, the focal point of Maya identity has remained the local community or *municipio*. It is through affiliation with a *municipio* that Indians distinguish themselves, even from outsiders who speak the same language. Social and cultural elements combine, adapt, become emphasized and assimilated from *municipio* to *municipio* in a manner that has been likened to a kaleidoscope (Nash 1969:35). The significance of the *municipio*, as reflected in Highland Maya clothing, has been aptly described by Lathbury: "Costume is a visual representation of a community and in abstract it incorporates certain ideas the inhabitants hold about themselves, their relationship to the universe and the world around them" (1974:5).

Today in communities such as Santiago Atitlán, Comalapa, Cotzal, Chajul, and Nebaj, the active role played by many of the Maya inhabitants in the national liberation movement has added a decisively political dimension to the symbolism of traditional costume. Recognizing that their garments mark them as targets for violent governmental reprisals, many Maya from these areas have begun to leave their native dress behind when traveling outside of their villages (Milton Jamail: personal communication 1981).

STYLE IN TWENTIETH-CENTURY GUATEMALAN WEAVING.
Throughout the Highlands, Maya weaving is still done principally to produce garments for men's and women's traditional costume, called *traje*. The basic garments that make up a woman's *traje* are a type of loose-fitting, sleeveless, upper garment called a *huipil*, a skirt (*corte, morga,* or *refajo*), a hair decoration (*cinta* or *tocoyal*), a sash (*faja*), a shawl (*perraje* or *rebozo*), and certain multipurpose accessory textiles (*tzutes* and *servilletas*). Where men's traditional costume is still worn, it can include a shirt (*camisa*), trousers

(*pantalones* or *calzones*), sash (*banda*), tunic (*capixay*), jacket (*cotón* or *saco*), and carrying bag (*bolsa* or *moral*). In some areas woolen blankets may be worn wrapped around the body (*poncho*) or as a type of kilt or apron over the trousers. Men also wear *tzutes* and *servilletas* but theirs always differ from those of the women of their village. Men and women either go barefoot or wear leather sandals with rubber soles made from automobile tires. The *huipil, banda, servilleta, tzute,* and *perraje* or *rebozo* are usually woven on the backstrap loom, whereas the others are generally foot loomed. These basic garments are modified to create distinctive styles and substyles from region to region, village to village, and among different social groups within the same village.

The term style as it is used in this study is defined as a particular constellation of the elements of shape, texture, color, and pattern that incorporates but is not limited to the dictates of medium, utilitarian function, or technological process. In the following pages the elements of shape, texture, color, and pattern, as they create stylistic differences in Guatemalan textiles, will be described and illustrated.

SHAPE. Most Guatemalan garments and accessory textiles are square or rectangular and are made from either a single length of fabric or several pieces joined together with little cutting or tailoring. If we consider that it may take a woman three months of fairly steady work to weave a *huipil* on the backstrap loom once it has been set up and warped, it is not surprising that as little of the fabric as possible is cut and discarded as scrap. The overall square or rectangular shape of the textile is then varied by the way in which it is arranged on the body or otherwise used.

A *huipil* usually lacks set-in sleeves and is made from one to three rectangular panels of cloth. In some villages several types are made for daily and ceremonial wear. The ceremonial *huipiles* tend to be stylistically more conservative than those woven for secular use. Most *huipiles* are still woven on the backstrap loom. They may reach from anywhere between just below the bust to the ankle in length and from just below the shoulder to the wrist in width. They may be worn either loose or tucked into the skirt.

Skirts range from knee- to ankle-length and can be as simple as a single piece of fabric from four to twelve yards long wrapped around the body or tucked or folded at the top and held in place by a sash. Another type of skirt, called *plegado* ("pleated"), is gathered at the waist with a drawstring. In some cases, two pieces of the same fabric may be joined to lengthen the skirt, or the selvages may be sewn together to form a large tube. These tube skirts are worn in a variety of ways, with the excess material arranged in folds or pleats in front or back.

A *perraje* is a length of fabric worn by women of many villages either around the shoulders as a shawl or folded and carried on the head until needed. Osborne reports that in Santa Cruz del Quiché and Tajumulco the folded *perraje* is worn over the left shoulder to indicate that a woman is unmarried and over the right to signify that she is married (Osborne 1965:113).

The *tzutes* and the smaller *servilletas* ("napkin" in Spanish) are uniformly rectangular or square and are constructed of one piece of fabric or two pieces of equal size joined at the center. *Tzutes* are folded and arranged in different ways to serve as head coverings, as wraps for ceremonial staffs, or as slings for carrying babies, wood, or produce. These cloths can also be used to wrap bundles, to cover tortillas, and to wear as shoulder wraps.

Indian women arrange and decorate their long hair in many different ways as markers of village affiliation, age, and marital status. Woven bands, ribbons, woolen cords (*tupi* or *tocoyal*), or broad pieces of cloth up to ten yards long can be braided into the hair, wrapped halo-fashion around the head, as at Santiago Atitlán, or folded to form a head covering, as at Zacualpa. Long, multicolored bands of silk or rayon with elaborate pompons at the ends, which are commercially woven in Totonicapán, have become popular in many Highland villages. Still, these bands are manipulated in many ways: twisted, wrapped, and knotted around the hair; straight on the head; or tilted to one side or the other.

Figure 5. Reconstruction of painted mural from Cawek Palace, Utatlán. Drawing by K. Kurbjuhn and Dwight D. Wallace from *The Quiché Mayas of Utatlán: The Evolution of a Highland Guatemala Kingdom,* by Robert M. Carmack. Copyright 1981 by the University of Oklahoma Press.

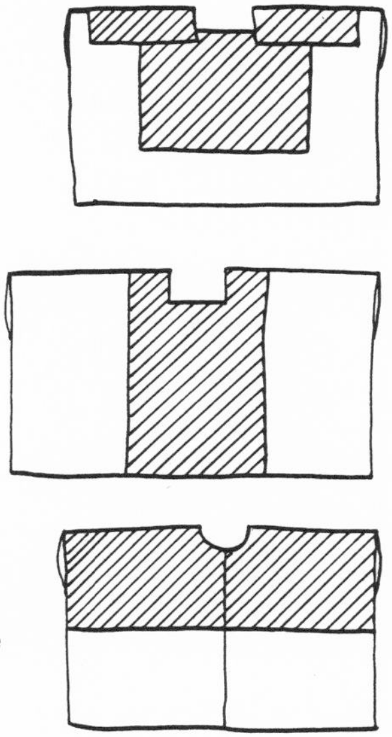

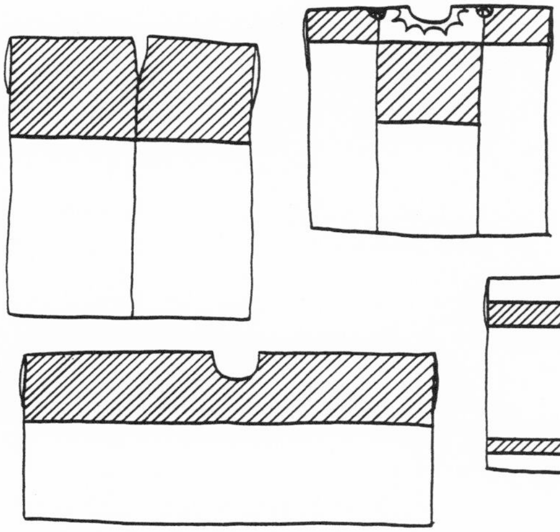

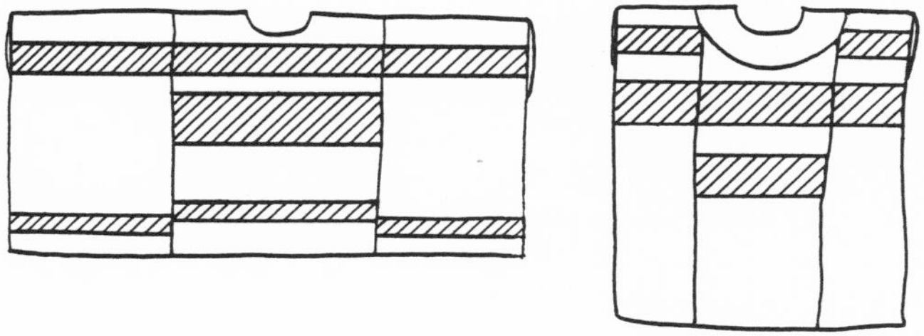

Figure 6. Some examples of one-, two-, and three-panel *huipil* construction. Shaded areas indicate allover supplementary weft patterning.

TEXTURE. Texture, the smoothness or roughness of the fabric, depends upon the type of fiber used, the evenness of the spin, the weaving technique employed, and the tightness of the weave. The ground fabric in Guatemalan textiles is almost always cotton. The exceptions are woolen blankets, jackets, overtrousers, or tunics. Handspun cotton, for example, whether the natural-brown (*Gossypium mexicanum tod.*, called *cuyuscate* in Guatemala), or natural-white (*Gossypium hirsutum l.*,) generally imparts a somewhat coarser texture to the fabric than the very tight and evenly spun machine-made threads. An especially skillful spinner can often match these qualities, however, making it difficult to distinguish handspun yarns from the commercial varieties. Some commercial cottons are mercerized (treated with a solution of caustic soda) and are stronger, smoother to the touch, and shinier than unmercerized threads. *Lustrina*, a cotton embroidery thread, is so shiny that it is often used in place of more expensive silk in contemporary weaving. Pattern yarns used in brocading, also called supplementary wefts, exhibit greater variety in fibers than those used for ground fabrics and hence a greater variety in texture. Guatemalan weavers take full advantage of the striking contrasts in texture between wool and acrylic, mercerized and unmercerized cottons, silks, and rayons, sometimes using several types of yarn in a single piece. Different textures can also be created by varying the way in which supplementary wefts are laid into the fabric as it is being woven. For instance, supplementary wefts may be pulled tight so that they just skim the surface of the fabric, or they may be "picked up" to produce a pile and an overall carpetlike effect.

COLOR. Color is the single most striking feature of Guatemalan textiles and a weaver's aesthetic sense is often judged by her peers according to the combination of colors she chooses. When a weaver from San Antonio Aguas Calientes, in the department of Sacatepéquez, is commissioned to weave a *huipil* for someone else, the client picks the pattern, but the weaver reserves the right to choose the colors (Lathbury 1974:16). Stylistic variables of color usage include the number of colors, the particular hues combined, the placement of colors in the ground fabric or in patterns applied to it, and the sequence (or lack of sequence) in which the colors are laid into the pattern.

Lila O'Neale (1945) reported only about twelve colors used by Indian weavers in Highland Guatemala, despite the fact that more than twenty had been available from the factory at Cantel since 1936 for professional dyers of Salcajá, San Cristóbal, and Totonicapán. In the early part of the century, cotton dyes were still obtained from plants and animals — red from the cochineal insect, blue and black from the indigo plant, a dark reddish brown from brazilwood, and a soft rosy purple from a Pacific coast mollusk (*Purpura patula pansa*). The rare and highly esteemed purple dye was reserved for textiles of the upper classes, and it is possible that the fondness of contemporary weavers for purple commercial yarns harks back to its association with elevated social status.

Osborne has suggested that the predominance of red, yellow, black, and white in *huipiles* may have originated with the Precolumbian association of these colors with the east, south, west, and north respectively (Osborne 1965:31). Although knowledge of such color symbolism may be retained by a few weavers, it is clear that color choice is guided primarily by individual aesthetic preference and village tradition.

In recent years, as the spectrum of relatively colorfast commercially dyed yarn, both domestic and imported, has expanded, so too has the "palette" of the Maya weaver. Particularly evident in the past twenty years is a general trend toward a greater number of colors of high value (lightness) and of high chroma (saturation), harmoniously combined within a single textile. The typical juxtaposition in a given textile of opposite or contrasting colors, such as red and green, lends a quality of vibrancy to the piece. *Huipiles*, usually the most elaborately decorated item of the native costume, display this type of color usage most clearly. Weavers in San Antonio Aguas Calientes state that the use of expensive embroidery yarns together with a great number of colors in a *huipil* is an indication of wealth (Lathbury 1974:60). The brilliantly colored *huipiles* favored by the younger generation in many villages are worn alongside the more subtly colored ones of the mothers and grandmothers.

PATTERN. Pattern in Guatemalan weaving can best be understood through a consideration of the various levels at which it can be created in any one textile. Five distinct levels of patterning can be examined. The first is the patterning made by the specific weaving technique employed in the ground fabric, which is either left plain or used as the background for other decorations. Although the pattern created by the ground-fabric weave is apparent only upon close inspection, it does provide clues toward the classification of styles and their development through time.

In the simplest type of loomed weave, defined as plain weave (over-one-under-one technique), a single weft element is passed alternately over one warp, or static element, and under the next, until all of the warps on the loom have been crossed, at which point the weft is passed through the warps in the opposite direction, each pass of the weft adding to the length of the growing fabric. There are many variations on this simple weave, several of which are utilized in Guatemalan weaving.

If there are more wefts than warps per inch and the wefts are tightly battened, the result is a weft-faced fabric. Conversely, warp-faced fabrics have concealed wefts and more warps than wefts per inch. A decorative ridge can be formed by using a thicker warp in a weft-faced fabric or a thicker weft in a warp-faced fabric. This technique is called ribbing and is best described in terms that explain whether the fabric is warp- or weft-faced. The expressions warp-wise (or vertical) ribbing and weft-wise (or horizontal) ribbing are probably the clearest (Emery 1966:87). Variations of plain weave are done on both backstrap and foot looms.

In twill weaves, the wefts do not cross alternate warps in over-one-under-one, plain weave fashion. Rather, they float over groups of warps, and adjacent wefts do not float over the same group of warps. For example, in one of the many types of plain twill, a weft will cross under two warps and over two warps. In the next pass of the weft, the warps will be paired differently. The effect is a diagonal alignment of the weft floats. In Highland Guatemala, plain twills are produced on the backstrap loom, but the more complicated herringbone and diamond twills are made only on the treadle loom.

Two backstrap-loomed fabric structures that are not plain weaves and are much less widely used are plain gauze weave for *huipiles* and veils, and a belt or sash technique called warp-faced alternating float weave. As the name implies, plain gauze weave is an open weave. In this technique, pairs of warps are twisted together as the weaving proceeds. First, the pair is twisted in one direction and the weft is passed between them. Then the pair is twisted back to its original position for the passing of another weft. It is then twisted again before the passing of the weft, and so on. Close examination of the face of a fabric in plain gauze weave will reveal that the same warp will always be the upper of the twisted warps. In warp-faced alternating float weave, a pattern is created by floating certain warps over wefts, but the body of the cloth is constructed predominantly by the warp-faced plain weave technique.

A second method of patterning, in conjunction with ground fabric patterning, is that in which designs are incorporated into textiles by the use of solidly colored warps and wefts to produce stripes, checks, and plaids, and also by a technique known as *ikat* (*jaspeado* in Spanish). *Ikat* involves the systematic tie-dyeing of groups of warps or wefts, usually cotton, before they are woven into the fabric. Skirts and other textiles with *ikat* patterning are called *jaspeados*. Many of the *jaspe* designs are specifically named, such as *jaspe botado* ("horizontal jaspe"), *rama* ("branch"), *liras* ("lyres"), *muñequitos* ("little dolls"), *jarros* ("jars"), *petateados* ("matlike designs"), and *cadenas* ("chains") (Dietrich, Erickson, and Younger 1979:62). Most of the *jaspeados* used in highland Guatemala today are produced in the factories of Salcajá, Quezaltenango, San Cristóbal Totonicapán, Totonicapán, Huehuetenango, Santiago Atitlán, and Sololá.

A third form of patterning in Guatemalan textiles is accomplished by a technique called supplementary weft patterning or, more commonly, brocade, in which supplementary yarns that are not essential to the structure of the fabric are incorporated into it during the weaving process in order to generate designs. These designs may appear to be identical on both sides of the fabric (double-faced), or they may appear on only one side (single-faced).

Seemingly endless varieties of animal, plant, and geometric design motifs are brocaded into either plain cloth or cloth with warp or weft designs. Since Precolumbian times, the bird motif has been among the most popular. This figure is elaborated according to the types and positions of the wings and tail, and in terms of readily identifiable traits, such as ducklike or roosterlike silhouette or bent-necked, humpbacked, or double-headed shapes. Many types of horses, monkeys, dogs, lions, human forms, and fanciful creatures also find their way into this brocaded detail. Geometric motifs, either worked separately or in combination with representational motifs, are prevalent and include diamonds, zigzags, chevrons, lozenges, frets, star shapes, and stylized representations of the sun.

On *huipiles*, generally the most heavily decorated textiles, the most common layout of design motifs is a series of horizontal bands often highlighted by a distinctive *mano* ("shoulder band") and/or a *pecho* ("breast band"). In some *municipios* the sequencing of motif bands is commonly reflected along the horizontal axis at the shoulder so that when the *huipil* is worn an identical pattern appears in front and back. In other cases the design field reflects along both horizontal and vertical axes creating a four-part overall patterning. Figure 6 shows some of the most common forms of *huipil* construction and design layout.

Embroidery (stitchery applied to a finished fabric with a sewing needle by hand or machine) is a fourth technique for creating design motifs and decorative patterns in Guatemalan weaving. Either as a purely decorative element, or as functional stitching that joins pieces of cloth, embroidery allows a range of design possibility unrestricted by the grid pattern of the weave structure. As a result, curvilinear and free-form designs not suited to the technique of brocading are typically embroidered. Embroidery is used principally to decorate armholes, necklines, and fabric joins, but in some villages, such as San Mateo Ixtatán, it is the principal technique used in the decoration of *huipiles*. The wide range of embroidery stitches represented in the Highland Guatemalan textile collections treated here is shown in Figure 7. Each village specializes in the use of one or more embroidery stitches, as is the case in the specialized use of supplementary weft techniques.

A fifth form of textile patterning in Highland Guatemala can be accomplished through the application of factory-made trims. Velvet, lace, crocheted yarn edging, plain and machine-embroidered ribbon, bias tape, and natural-colored or dyed muslin are examples that have become increasingly available and widely used in the past twenty years. In addition to their most common usage for neckline and armhole trims, taffeta, velvet, or cotton cloth are made into rosettes to adorn the shoulders at the front and back of some *huipiles*. In some cases, bands of commercial ribbons sewn onto a *huipil* have completely replaced handworked decorations.

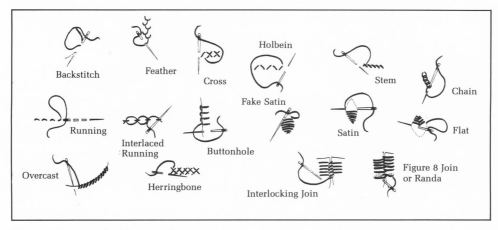

Figure 7. Some embroidery stitches used in Maya weaving.

Men and women from Santiago
Atitlán or a Lake Atitlán village, ca.
1910. Taylor Museum photo archives,
2785.

DESCRIPTIVE CATALOGUE
Twentieth-Century Guatemalan Weaving

IN THIS CHAPTER, Maya textiles of Highland Guatemala from the Taylor Museum's Edith Bayles Ricketson collection are presented and compared to similar pieces in the collections of nine other institutions and individuals. Community styles and intravillage substyles are discussed with reference to the stylistic elements detailed in Part I — shape, color, texture, and pattern — and apparent stylistic trends are identified whenever possible. Because the *huipil* is the most elaborately decorated and best represented of all the costume textiles in the collections, it is the focus of the discussion.

Both stylistic stability and change are products of the interaction between the weaver and his or her social universe. The need to communicate, to share the message embodied in a garment, whether it signifies community or social class affiliations, constrains the weaver's expression. However, stylistic rules are not rigidly fixed and are continually manipulated in such a way as to satisfy both traditional meanings and the need for individual creativity.

Relatively little is known about the agents and processes of stylistic change in Guatemalan textiles, although a wealth of information is available on the technical aspects of weaving. Some of the questions to be investigated include: Who are the innovators in a given community? Are they primarily individuals, families, or nonrelated weavers working together and sharing ideas? What social factors condition the acceptance or rejection of specific innovations in weaving styles? For instance, Lathbury reports that in San Antonio Aguas Calientes: "When one weaver experiments with color, others carefully watch, and by gossip or direct discussion, decide to ignore it or to follow suit" (1974:64).

At the intercommunity level we need to investigate such issues as the effects on weaving styles of intermarriage, political strife, and marketing systems. The work of Carol Smith on marketing networks in the western Highlands, for example, provides a provocative beginning for a study of the relationship between stylistic change in weaving and intervillage commerce (Smith 1972, 1973, 1975, 1976). In conclusion, formal stylistic analysis is not an end in itself, but represents a means toward furthering our understanding of the relationship between textile arts and the cultural and social context within which they are created.

Note: If figure is not near the text where it is mentioned, it can be found by checking "Index of figures" on page 115.

Figure 10. Huipil from San Miguel Chicaj, ca. 1970, Gordon Frost Collection.

BAJA VERAPAZ
Rabinal, San Miguel Chicaj, San Gabriel Pansuj

People of the neighboring valley communities of Rabinal, San Miguel Chicaj, and San Gabriel Pansuj (a hamlet of San Miguel Chicaj) speak a dialect of Quiché Maya known as Achi or Rabinal. At the time of the conquest Rabinal was an important political center, ethnically unique, but subordinate to the Quiché lords of Utatlán. In

Figure 11. Huipil from San Miguel Chicaj, ca. 1940, Penn 42-35-408.

Figure 12. Modern *huipil* from San Miguel Chicaj, ca. 1976. AMNH 65/5882.

1537, Fray Bartolomé de las Casas and his companion, Fray Pedro de Angilo, consolidated all the native population of the area that had not already dispersed at a site about five miles from the present-day location of the Rabinal municipal center. San Miguel Chicaj and San Gabriel Pansuj are villages that directly descend from Rabinal. The name Chicaj is derived from two Quiché words (*chi* = in; *caj* = sky) and was given to the town because its patron saint, Saint Michael, was believed to have come from the sky. The Rabinal area is renowned for the production of carved and painted gourd containers, lustrous red ceramic vessels, and palm mats. These products, along with oranges and avocados, are traded throughout the Guatemalan Highlands.

The shared cultural and political heritage of the three communities is amply reflected in their weaving, particularly in the cut and design of the *huipil*. Based on information gathered from the collections studied, it is clear that at least two styles of *huipil* have been made since the turn of the century. One is a loosely woven ceremonial (or Mass) *huipil*, consisting of three fabric panels. The other is a single-breadth *huipil* made on an unusually wide backstrap loom.

The Mass *huipil* (Figure 8) is worn draped over the head (thus satisfying the Catholic standard for religious reverence) and falls so that the circular neck opening frames the face. Pouches are formed by joining the corners of the fabric at the ends of the sleeves, and in them women may carry home small purchases from town after Mass on Sunday (Osborne 1965:107). Judging from examples studied, the style of the Mass *huipil* appears to have changed little in the past seventy years. It typically features dense, predominantly red banding on the central panel and a separate design band running across the bottom. Brocading on the side panel, when it occurs, tends to be sparse. Horizontal ribbing (cf. p. 31), or bands of closely battened-down wefts, complete the consistently horizontal patterning. Two variants of this style, one (Figure 9) dating to the early part and the other to the middle of this century, share a much more isolated treatment of motifs and a balanced usage of green and/or blue with red and yellow. Design motifs for all Mass *huipiles* include simple geometrics — serrate or stepped diamonds, chevrons, zigzags, and blocks.

Design of the daily *huipil*, less restrained by the stylistic conventions imposed upon ceremonial garments, is more variable from town to town, and even within the same town. From San Miguel Chicaj alone, three substyles of the daily *huipil* from the middle and late periods of this century are represented in the collections. In contrast to the Mass style, decorative patterning on the daily *huipil* employs vertical placement of motifs in the fabric weave or in brocading. While the literature lacks descriptions of early twentieth-century *huipiles*, sources indicate that *huipiles* of the type shown (Figure 10) have been common in all three villages since the 1940s (Wood and Osborne 1966:144-145; Petterson 1976:80-81; Bunch and Bunch 1977:25). The red-plaid style daily *huipil* of San Miguel (Figure 11), represented in two mid-century collections, was also noted by O'Neale (1945) as typical of Rabinal weaving during the same period, but no longer appears to be used. It provides an interesting example of stylistic transformation, combining elements of the modern daily *huipil* styles with elements from the Mass *huipil*. Specifically, the colors and design motifs in horizontal bands, like those of the Mass style, are superimposed upon a background of bold, vertical stripes that have been transformed into repeating vertical zigzags brocaded on the modern daily *huipil* (Figure 10). The latter piece incorporates the dominant blue color scheme and repetitive patterning of the other modern daily *huipil* (Figure 12) while retaining red and yellow accents from the plaid-style daily *huipil*.

CHIMALTENANGO

Acatenango, San Antonio Nejapa

Cakchiquel-speaking towns, Acatenango and San Antonio Nejapa have identical costumes owing to the fact that Nejapa was annexed in 1934 to the *municipio* of Acatenango (Delgado 1963:280). The name Acatenango is derived from a Nahuatl word meaning "in the enclosure of reeds."

The *huipil* of these villages is distinctive for its combination of three-panel construction, striped ground of either red and white or red with natural brown cotton, and thick picked-pile brocading, mainly in red. The typical "cross" layout of the brocaded patterns is illustrated by the Taylor Museum's *huipil* from Acatenango (Figure 14). In 1963 Delgado documented a new *huipil* style, influenced by the *huipil* of the departmental capital of Chimaltenango and generally more poorly woven than that described above. The new style incorporates a blue ground fabric; it was not represented in the collections studied.

Figure 13. Man's jacket from San Miguel Chicaj, ca. 1930. TM 712.

CHIMALTENANGO

San Juan Comalapa

Comalapa is situated at the base of a mountaintop archaeological site known as Chij-Xot or Chuitinamit. A Late Postclassic stronghold of the Cakchiquel, Chij-Xot was conquered by Pedro de Alvarado's forces in 1527, and the village of Comalapa, then called San Juan Comalapa, was established near its present location. The name Comalapa is a Spanish translation of the Chij-Xot expression meaning "in" or "on a *comal*" (a flat ceramic griddle for cooking tortillas). Baskets made in Comalapa are traded in the local markets and in the city of Antigua, Guatemala.

The most marked stylistic change in Comalapa weaving has occurred in the *huipil*. According to Bjerregaard (1977b), the transformation of the *huipil* has been in progress since as early as the 1920s. Comalapa *huipiles* in collections from the 1930s and 1940s such as the Taylor Museum's (Figure 15), document this change when compared to those of later collections. The earlier *huipil* style is most easily identified by its red shoulder band in weft-faced plain weave technique and a limited repertory of geometric and animal motifs arranged in horizontal bands and separated by thin stripes of contrasting colors. Handspun natural white, brown (*cuyuscate*), or white and brown checked cotton make up the ground fabric, while silk or a combination of silk and wool form the brocaded patterns.

Modern style *huipiles,* of comparable quality to earlier style weavings, are strikingly different in their use of materials, colors, and design motifs. Handspun natural-colored yarns, except in some of the most prized pieces, have been replaced by commercially spun and dyed cotton yarns. Sometimes white or dyed brown is chosen for the ground fabric, in imitation of the traditional style; but dark blue and green are also used. Shiny cotton embroidery thread (*lustrina*) supplements the more costly silk floss. Although the red shoulder band is usually preserved, it is often

Figure 16. Detail of *huipil* fabric from San Juan Comalapa, ca. 1970. Gordon Frost Collection.

Figure 22. *Huipil* from San Martín Jilotepeque, ca. 1900. Lowie 3-243.

produced by a simple plain weave technique that requires less thread than the previous weft-faced style. The small number of traditional design motifs has expanded and changed in character due to the widespread use of commercial pattern books from southern Mexico (Figures 16, 17). Parrots, rabbits, complex flowering vines, letters, and even reindeer are executed in many colors and shades to produce a three-dimensional effect never attempted in aboriginal weaving. Two weaving cooperatives in Comalapa produce these modern-style *huipiles* for native consumption, thereby taking weaving out of its traditional place in the household. The stylistic transformation of the *huipil* needs to be studied in relation to this social and economic change.

In addition to the daily *huipiles* described above, one exquisite example of a *cofradía huipil* was located in the Tulane University's Middle American Research Institute collection (Figure 18). Made of a single panel of natural brown cotton, this *huipil* is brocaded in a greater number and more varied kinds of silk motifs than any other daily *huipil* in the collections studied. A double-headed bird at the center of the breast and four sets of ribbons flowing from the neckline add to its regal character. This *huipil* style has not been documented previously in the literature.

Today, *huipil* styles from a number of Highland villages are woven by Comalapa women for sale and for their own use. This eclecticism is the result of expanding market influences channeled through the weavers' cooperatives. Because these cooperatives have fostered social and economic independence as well as unity among Maya peoples, the government has targeted them for repression. One co-op leader, now in exile, has traveled internationally, exhibiting and selling her weavings (Milton Jamail: personal communication 1981).

CHIMALTENANGO
San José Poaquil

San José Poaquil lies directly north of the village of Comalapa, from which it is descended. The traditional *huipil* for everyday wear (Figure 19) is virtually identical to that of Comalapa, except that it is not tucked into the skirt, nor is it usually sewn up the sides. Examples in the collections studied also document the same trend in modern *huipil* style described for Comalapa except that black velvet appliqué has been added at the neckline and armholes in the *huipil* style typical of San José Poaquil weaving. An extreme but delightful example of the modern-style *huipil* boasts a multicolored *pecho* ("breast band") of curly-headed cherubs riding donkeys (Figure 20).

CHIMALTENANGO
San Martín Jilotepeque

San Martín Jilotepeque is a large Cakchiquel-speaking community of nearly 30,000 people. Encompassed within its northeast border is the important Late Postclassic (1200-1524 A.D.) site of Chaupec Quecahol Nimaabah or Jilotepeque Viejo. Incorrectly identified by the Spanish chronicler Fuentes y Guzmán in the seventeenth century as Mixcu, and subsequently as Mixco Viejo, the site was thought to have been inhabited by the Pokomam Maya (Fox 1978:203). Recently, ethnohistoric documents have revealed the true identity of the site as a Cakchiquel center and fort directly ancestral to the present municipality of San Martín Jilotepeque (Carmack 1981, Fox 1978). The name Jilotepeque was given to the town by Mexican colonists in the sixteenth century and means, in the Nahuatl language, "hill of the tender corn."

The *huipil* of Jilotepeque (Figure 21) is characterized by two-panel construction and a pattern of five major horizontal bands with alternating motif fillers. When draped on the body, the back and front patterning is virtually identical. *Pechos* ("breast bands") usually consisting of chevron or zigzag patterns bordered by narrower bands of the same motifs, are found at the center front and back. Another Jilotepeque trademark is the small dot or dot-cluster motif within the bands surrounding the *pecho*, found on almost all *huipiles* made prior to 1940. Before 1930, the ground fabric was handspun white cotton (Figure 22), but since that time dark blue commercially dyed and spun cotton has become increasingly popular. Brocaded designs, although still executed in no more than four or five colors per *huipil*, incorporate new shades such as pink and turquoise rather than the strictly red, yellow, and blue typical of the earlier pieces. A trend toward dense brocading with contiguous design bands covering the entire surface of the *huipil* was noted in examples from the collections dating from the latter half of the century. The traditional dot motif was not present in most post-1940 examples and the plain red lines of the early twentieth-century *huipil* have become embellished with commercial trims of lace, velvet, or taffeta ribbon. Some modern *huipiles* (Figure 23) are joined at the center seam by multicolored embroidery in a *randa* ("figure-eight stitch").

A rare example of the mourning *huipil* in the University of Alberta collections (Figure 24) differs from all of the daily *huipiles* described above in having a monochromatic color scheme and tiny design motifs, delicately brocaded.

Figure 23. Huipil from San Martín Jilotepeque, ca. 1970. Gordon Frost Collection.

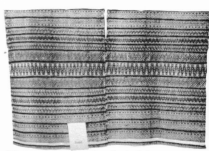

Figure 24. Mourning huipil from San Martín Jilotepeque, ca. 1975. Alberta 75.2.21.

CHIMALTENANGO

Santa Apolonia

The Cakchiquel *municipio* of Santa Apolonia produces strong utility baskets and red ceramic vessels in a variety of shapes and sizes. Pottery making has remained a specialty of Santa Apolonia women since Precolumbian times.

Three types of *huipil* are represented in the collections — a simple work *huipil*, a *cofradía huipil*, and a daily *huipil*. In contrast to the Taylor Museum work *huipil*, undecorated except for some overcast stitchery at the neckline and armhole openings, the *cofradía huipil* in the collection has a well-defined yoke of fine silk brocade (Figure 25). The opening under the front design area is outlined in silk embroidery and facilitates nursing. Fretted diamonds and x's are typical motifs of the *municipio* of Tecpán, that borders Santa Apolonia on the west, while the horselike creature with uplifted foreleg seen on the *cofradía huipil* of Tecpán closely resembles the motif found on the *cofradía huipil* of Comalapa, situated to the east of Santa Apolonia (Figure 18).

Contemporary *huipiles* for everyday use are represented in the Gordon Frost collection (Figure 26). They are most unusual in their lack of a well-defined pattern area or symmetry in either the placement of design motifs or in the use of color. Bright orange, green, blue, and violet cotton (*lustrina*) embroidery contrasts with the

Figure 26. Huipil from Santa Apolonia, ca. 1970. Gordon Frost Collection.

pastel-colored reversal brocading of the Taylor Museum *cofradía huipil*. Vertical zigzags form a *mano* ("shoulder band"), but the most distinctive motif on these modern *huipiles* is the cluster of stacked triangles. A ground fabric of vertically striped red, yellow, and natural brown cotton used in the two ceremonial *huipiles* in the Frost collection offers further evidence of stylistic exchange between Santa Apolonia and Tecpán.

CHIMALTENANGO

Tecpán

Tecpán, a city of more than 12,000 people, is situated next to the Precolumbian capital of the powerful Cakchiquel Maya, Iximché. Conquered by Spaniards under the direction of Pedro de Alvarado in 1524, the town was renamed by Mexican mercenaries. Tecpán means "royal residence" in the Nahuatl language. Along with the traditional crops of corn and beans, Tecpán produces rice, alfalfa, and wheat, which is ground into flour in local mills. Its forests yield wood for construction and cabinet making.

There are two principal styles of *huipil* for daily wear, both constructed of two fabric panels joined at the center. One has a predominantly white ground (Figure 27); the other is striped in natural brown and dyed red and yellow cotton. The white style is worn either alone, for work, or underneath the more costly and heavily decorated striped *huipil* for added warmth in cold weather. Design motifs are characteristically bold and include fretted or serrate diamonds, serrate lozenges, zigzags, chevrons, and a two-part bird with an upturned tail. These two styles and a more richly decorated three-panel version of the striped style, for ceremonial occasions, have been worn since at least the early part of this century.

Since 1940, however, several new *huipil* varieties have developed. One such style, shown in Figure 28, is characterized by contiguous design bands including a *mano* ("shoulder band") and *pecho* ("breast band") with large zigzags and chevron motifs. Ground fabrics may be of the traditional striped type, but bright blue, green, and even pink commercial cottons are employed. Symmetry in patterning along vertical and horizontal axes as well as in color placement is more pronounced than in the earlier pieces. A more radical departure from tradition is exemplified in Figure 29, where free-form European-style motifs, copied from pattern books, are incorporated, somewhat uneasily, into the design bands.

The stiff, wide woman's belt exhibits less drastic stylistic changes than the *huipiles*, and even today is worn wound around the waist until it reaches just under the bustline.

Figure 28. Huipil from Tecpán, ca. 1970. Gordon Frost Collection.

CHIMALTENANGO

San Andrés Itzapa

The costume of San Andrés Itzapa, a little-known Cakchiquel-speaking community, has not been previously documented in the literature. The *huipiles* in the Taylor Museum collection (Figure 30) are typical of a style of daily *huipil* that originated in the 1930s and is still woven along with newer variations in San Antonio Aguas Calientes, Sacatepéquez. Bordering Itzapa on the east, Aguas Calientes

Figure 9. Mass *huipil* from Rabinal,
ca. 1900, Lowie 3-130.

Figure 8. Mass *huipil* from
San Miguel Chicaj, ca. 1930. TM
718.

Figure 15. Woman's costume from
San Juan Comalapa, ca. 1930.
Huipil: TM 773, Skirt: TM 770,
Sash: TM 761.

Figure 14. *Huipil* fabric from Acatenango, ca. 1930. TM 715.

Figure 20. Huipil from San José Poaquil, ca. 1970. Gordon Frost Collection.

Figure 21. Huipil from San Martín Jilotepeque, ca. 1930. TM 613.

Figure 18. Cofradía huipil from San Juan Comalapa, ca. 1930. MARI G.15.2, 41-59 B.

Figure 27. Woman's costume from Tecpán, ca. 1930. *Huipil:* TM 772, Work *huipil:* TM 764, Woman's sash: TM 762.

Figure 25. Detail of *cofradía huipil* from Santa Apolonia, ca. 1900-1920. TM 607.

Figure 30. *Huipiles* from San Andrés Itzapa, ca. 1930. Left, TM 608, right, TM 610.

Figure 31. Cofradía huipil from San Andrés Itzapa, ca. 1930. Penn 66-34-33.

Figure 33. Woman's costume from Palín, ca. 1930. *Huipil:* TM 611, Woman's sash: TM 831.

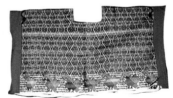

Figure 35. Huipil from Palín, ca. 1970. Penn 70-13-23a.

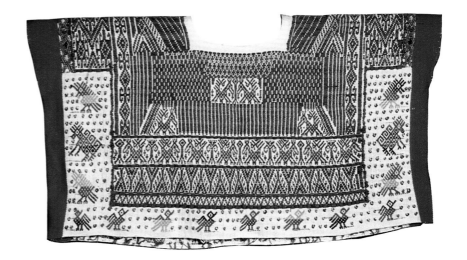

Figure 34. *Huipil* from Palín,
ca. 1970. Heard NA-CA-Gu-C-184.

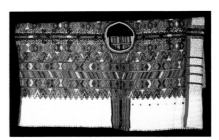

Figure 49. *Huipil* from San Pedro
Sacatepéquez, ca. 1970. UCLA
X76-1185, gift of Caroline and
Howard West.

Figure 38. *Cofradía huipil* from
Mixco, ca. 1910. TM 753.

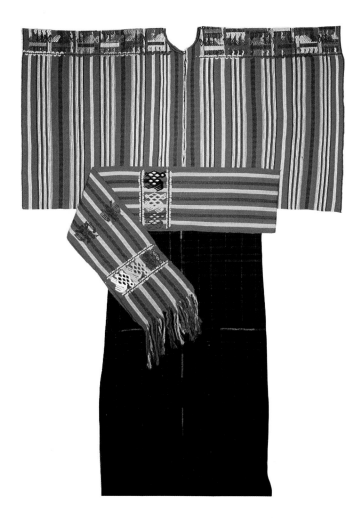

Figure 40. Woman's costume from San Juan Sacatepéquez, ca. 1930. *Huipil*: TM 1034, Sash: TM 1033, Skirt: TM 1035.

Figure 44. Woman's costume from San Pedro Sacatepéquez, ca. 1930. Fiesta *huipil*: TM 737, Sash: TM 741, Skirt: TM 745.

Figure 55. *Huipil* from Santo Tomás Chichicastenango, ca. 1975. Alberta 75.2.256.

Figure 60. *Huipil* from Joyabaj, ca. 1930. TM 619.

Figure 54. *Huipiles* and belt from Santo Tomás Chichicastenango, ca. 1930. *Huipil* (natural brown cotton): TM 623, Christening *huipil* (natural white cotton): TM 624, Sash: TM 626.

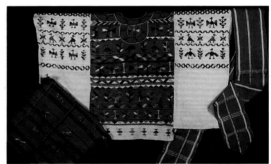

Figure 63. Woman's costume from San Juan Cotzal, ca. 1930. *Huipil*: TM 792, Sash: TM 779, *Servilleta*: TM 781.

is one of the most prolific weaving centers in Guatemala and is the probable source of these pieces. However, in the University of Pennsylvania collection is a distinctive style of *huipil* from San Andrés Itzapa (Figure 31) dating to roughly the same period as the Taylor Museum example. Its three-panel construction and lavish use of handwoven natural brown cotton (*cuyuscate*), silk floss, and ribbon trims identify it as a ceremonial garment.

CHIMALTENANGO Santa Cruz Balanyá

The name of this small village, located far off the beaten track, translates from the native Cakchiquel as "water of the tiger." The Taylor Museum's *huipil* (Figure 32) with its whimsical bird, butterfly, and floral embroidery, is unlike any other style in the region. Another distinctive feature is a technique locally called *chivo* ("goat"), by which weft threads are looped on the exterior of the garment. The textiles of this community have not been previously documented in the literature, nor were they represented in any of the other collections studied.

ESCUINTLA Palín

Palín is the only town in the industrialized department of Escuintla that has retained its Indian character. South of Palín the terrain drops abruptly to the coastal tropics; consequently, the region specializes in growing pineapples, papayas, and bananas. Palín women balance large baskets of these fruits and other prepared foods on their heads as they run to the railroad stop to sell them to passengers. The name Palín comes from the Pokomam term *palinja*, meaning "at the foot of the waters," in reference to the spectacular high waterfall at the outskirts of town.

The Palín *huipil* is easily identified by its unusually short length, single breadth of fabric, red warp-faced plain weave bands along the armholes and side seams, motifs striped in alternate colors, and its predominantly purple and red coloration. Despite its uniqueness, however, the *huipil* is not without stylistic variation. One well-documented change in the *huipil* took place between 1934 and 1944. In a so-called "decency decree," the dictator of Guatemala, Jorge Ubico, ordered the lengthening of the *huipil* so that the breasts would remain covered when the women raised their arms.

At least three different pattern layouts are represented in the collections. The first type, found only in collections dating between 1920 and 1950, features noncontiguous bands of design motifs either crossing the entire width of the *huipil* or forming a rectangular border of filler motifs (Figure 33). The most conservative substyle, remaining virtually unchanged since the 1920s, is exemplified in Figure 34. It is characterized by the architectural arrangement of design areas with specific motifs confined to particular areas of the design field. The large double-headed bird with a smaller one on its breast, for instance, is always centrally placed on the front and back of the garment. Lastly, in a modern *huipil* type, design patterning is simplified through the rejection of a single interlocking motif (Figure 35), but the traditional alternating bands of color are retained.

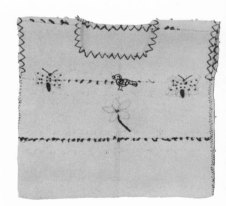

Figure 32. *Huipil* from Santa Cruz Balanyá, ca. 1930. TM 720.

The typical woman's belt of the the 1930-1940 period (Figure 33) is similar to those worn since at least 1960, except that the more modern examples are narrower and more colorful. In addition, rows of vertical zigzags have been added between the horizontal zigzags that are typical of the middle-period pieces.

GUATEMALA Mixco

When Alvarado conquered the fortified capital of the Pokomam people, at a site near the present town of Chinautla, Guatemala, the inhabitants were moved close to the modern capital of Guatemala City, where the town of Mixco was established. The town was named Mixcono, the Indian word for "place covered with clouds." Placed under the rule of Alvarado's Tlaxcalan Indian mercenaries from central Mexico, the inhabitants of Mixco exhibit distinctive Mexican racial and cultural features. For example, the woman's belt of Mixco, called *mixqueño*, is imported from Oaxaca, and the bulky woolen headdress of the woman's *cofradía* costume is a Mexican-influenced style.

The two-panel daily *huipil* of Mixco has a highly standardized pattern of horizontal banding, including a *mano* ("shoulder band"), identical front and back *pechos* ("breast bands"), and bottom border bands (Figure 36). A small repertory of geometric design motifs, featuring zigzags bordered by a checkerboard pattern, has characterized the *huipil* since the early part of the century (Figure 37). The only significant change has been the addition of red and yellow to the dark blue and lavender color scheme represented in the early twentieth-century pieces. The common use of a three-weft plain weave pattern for the ground fabric has also remained constant through time.

The oldest Mixco textile in the Taylor Museum collection is a three-panel *cofradía huipil* dating from around 1910 (Figure 38). Very different from the daily *huipil* in its cut and embroidery decoration, which includes small figures and lace and sequin trims, this *huipil* style has remained unchanged to the present day. A lace-trimmed shawl and a loosely woven white veil with white brocading, worn over a woolen headdress, complete the woman's *cofradía* costume. Brocading on one *cofradía* veil, located in the American Museum of Natural History collection and dating to the early part of this century, depicts a two-steeple church across its width. *Ikat*-patterned material in blue and white or more rarely yellow, red, blue, and white is gathered into a full, pleated skirt in the Spanish tradition.

Figure 36. Woman's costume from Mixco, ca. 1930. *Huipil* fabric: TM 1028, Sash: TM 1027, Skirt: TM 1031.

San Juan Sacatepéquez, San Pedro Sacatepéquez, San Pedro Chuarrancho, San Pedro Ayampuc

GUATEMALA

These Cakchiquel-speaking communities are situated to the north of Guatemala City and are related culturally and historically. San Juan and San Pedro Sacatepéquez are relatively new towns founded in the eighteenth century when a group of Maya from the area united to purchase the lands from the Spanish crown. At the end of the nineteenth century, Chuarrancho was actually annexed to San Pedro Sacatepéquez before regaining its independence as a *municipio* in the early twentieth century.

Another factor contributing to the stylistic uniformity in some costume textiles is the prolific output of the San Pedro Sacatepéquez backstrap weavers. Renowned for their weaving skill, these women produce *huipiles* on commission for surrounding villages or for sale to itinerant merchants. The traders may also peddle them through the marketplace at Guatemala City or as far away as Sololá (Anderson 1978:12). The development of the San Pedro Sacatepéquez textile trade and the extent of its influence on the weaving styles of recipient villages warrant further study.

From San Juan Sacatepéquez alone, five different types of *huipil* are represented in the collections. The first style, dating from the beginning of this century and shown in Figure 39, has simple bands of alternating geometric and figurative (horse) motifs in dark blue on a white cotton background. Three very different styles (ca. 1930) can be found in the collections — a striped *huipil* of red, yellow, lavender, and white with a brocaded *mano* ("shoulder band," Figure 40); a solid dark blue ground *huipil* brocaded across the width and across the shoulders (Figure 41); and a striped *huipil* of white and lavender with a lavender and red *mano*. In collections made after 1950, a fourth type of *huipil* is commonly found that resembles the red-striped style of the previous period. However, purple predominates over the yellow and red in the stripes of the ground fabric, and the brocaded motifs are larger and mainly yellow and purple (Figure 42). The same change in color scheme can also be noted in the women's wide belts. Finally, since at least 1920, San Juan weavers have made a three-panel *cofradía huipil* with a design area that, when laid out flat, forms a cross-symbol of the four directions or winds of the heavens (Rodas, Rodas, and Hawkins 1940) (Figure 43). Typical design motifs that appear in San Juan textiles are horses, double-headed birds, fretted diamonds, and a two-part bird with upraised tail and wing.

As is the case at San Juan, *huipiles* from San Pedro Sacatepéquez and a type made in San Pedro Chuarrancho favor red and lavender, color-banding of individual motifs, and mirror symmetry of brocaded patterning along the center seam of two-panel *huipiles*. The most common *huipil* style, more richly decorated for fiesta wear with silk, or in recent years, rayon, has been in use since at least 1910. It has large birds or horselike animals with fretted appendages, a unique tree motif centered on the breast and back, and a geometric *mano*. The brocading is a form of reversal weaving in which the pattern wefts are individually tufted on the front of the fabric to form a distinctive carpetlike texture (Figure 44). This technique has become exaggerated in some modern examples of this *huipil* style to such an extent that the detail inside a motif is entirely obscured (Figure 45). An exceptionally striking *huipil* in the Taylor Museum from San Pedro Chuarrancho (Figure 46) demonstrates the use of tufted-pile texturing in that village during the 1930s.

A second *huipil* style of San Pedro Sacatepéquez differs from the first not only in its almost exclusive use of geometric motifs, but in its single-faced float supplementary weft patterning. *Huipiles* of the period 1930-1940 from San Pedro Ayampuc (Figure 47) and San Pedro Chuarrancho provide examples of styles from which the geometric style common to all three communities in recent decades may have developed. The richly brocaded surfaces of these textiles, like their modern counterparts, are patterned in contiguous bands so that the ground fabric is almost entirely covered. In contrast, the 1930-period geometric *huipil* from San Pedro Sacatepéquez in the Taylor Museum (Figure 48) is decorated only with *manos*,

Figure 41. *Huipil* from San Juan Sacatepéquez, ca. 1930. MARI G.13.4, 35-6629.

Figure 42. *Huipil* from San Juan Sacatepéquez, ca. 1970. Heard NA-CA-Gu-C-131.

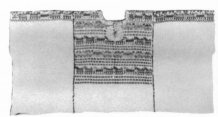

Figure 43. *Cofradía huipil* from San Juan Sacatepéquez, ca. 1930. TM 823.

Figure 50. Man's *cofradía tzute* from San Juan Sacatepéquez, ca. 1930. TM 822.

Santo Tomás Chichicastenango

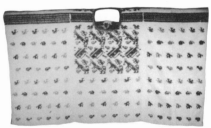

Figure 51. Cofradía huipil from San Pedro Sacatepéquez, ca. 1930. MARI G.13.4, 41-333.

Figure 52. Huipil from San Pedro Ayampuc, ca. 1930. TM 758.

pechos ("breast bands"), and isolated filler motifs. The geometric style *huipiles* of the post-1950 period (Figure 49) are dazzling in their use of as many as eight colors on a single piece, giving their wearers the appearance of a walking rainbow. The intervillage stylistic uniformity of the modern *huipiles* is striking and may be due to the necessity for standardization in the production of trade weavings. Other recent stylistic innovations found in these *huipiles* include a curious double exposure effect, created by superimposing two brocaded motifs, and the use of wide *randas* ("figure-eight stitches") down the center seam in bright, multicolored bands.

Evidence of diversification in weaving styles between San Pedro and San Juan Sacatepéquez is provided by a *cofradía huipil* from San Pedro (Figure 51) and a *huipil* from San Juan dating to the early twentieth century (Lowie 3-141, not illustrated). Although the latter differs in its construction of two rather than three panels, the colors, design motifs, and their pattern of arrangement are very similar.

In addition to the San Pedro Ayampuc *cofradía huipil* style noted above (Figure 47), two other types of daily *huipil* are represented in the Taylor Museum collection (Figures 52, 53). The *huipil* in Figure 52 is unusual for having a red ground, brocaded color scheme, and lack of color symmetry between the two panels.

EL QUICHÉ

Chichicastenango is perhaps the best known town in Guatemala because of its lively market and accessibility over paved roads. Each Thursday and Sunday, native traders and tourists flock to the marketplace in the central plaza. Despite such intensive commerce with outsiders, the Maxeños, as the natives of the town are called, are traditionalists. In general, contacts with outsiders are restricted to the narrow sphere of the marketplace and rarely penetrate the approximately fifty outlying hamlets which constitute the municipality. It is not uncommon to see a group of Maxeños burning *copal* ("pine pitch") incense and praying to their aboriginal deities on the steps of the large colonial church which dominates the plaza. The native language is Quiché.

Today women still wear the customary *traje* but only elderly men or those who hold a civil or religious office continue to do so. Changes in the *huipil* of Chichicastenango in the past fifteen to twenty years have been described by Conte (1974), Bjerregaard (1977b), and Siskin (1977). The older style, represented in the Taylor Museum (Figure 54) and still worn by older women, is made of three breadths of handspun white or natural brown cotton with picked-pile brocading in silk and/or wool. Upper-class ceremonial *huipiles* are predominantly purple rather than red and have more silk floss than woolen patterning (author's field data:1973). A special method of incorporating pattern wefts creates diagonal lines of brocading. When laid out flat the brocaded area forms a large cross, signifying the four winds or four directions, and the appliquéd neckline depicts the sun surrounded by four cloth, disklike "moons" (Rodas, Rodas and Hawkins 1940).

Modern *huipiles* differ in technique, materials, and patterns and maintain none of the symbolic content of the earlier style. A wide range of colors in *lustrina*, acrylic, orlon, and even metallic yarns are typical for pattern wefts while machine-milled cotton thread from Cantel has all but replaced the handspun ground fabric yarns of the past. A simplification of the previous brocading technique has changed the diagonal pattern to a vertical one. Large flowers and occasionally birds, copied from cross-stitch embroidery pattern books from Europe and Mexico, are the dominant motifs. The flowers are also embroidered on women's belts in satin stitch. Where geometric designs are used in *huipiles*, they are massive and simplified. If any cloth moons are used, there are only two; and the "sun" neckline design is often replaced by a ready-made floral embroidered collar. The *huipil* (Figure 55) is typical, and even includes the ultimate in modernity — a zippered neck opening.

The men's woolen pants and jacket (Figure 56) are woven on treadle looms and tailored locally. The garments are embroidered by townsmen with symbols of the sun, especially on the side flaps of the pant legs. These vary in elaborateness depending upon the age and rank of the wearer. Even on these garments, however, floral motifs and *quetzal* birds are not uncommon modern decorations. Four types of men's *tzutes*, worn on the head with a diagonal fold, are in the collections studied. These vary in color combinations and motifs, but the time period cannot be distinguished. The man's shoulder blanket, a product of the local treadle loom, is highly standardized in style and has remained virtually unchanged since the turn of the century.

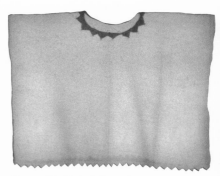

Figure 58. Huipil from Aguacatán, ca. 1900. Lowie 3-199.

EL QUICHÉ Chiché

Bordering Chichicastenango to the west and south is the Quiché municipality of Chiché. Its name means "in the woods." In addition to subsistence farming, the townspeople devote themselves to tanning, leatherwork, and the production of treadle-loomed woolens.

According to O'Neale (1945:256) the woman's *traje* is like that of Chichicastenango, but the white windowpane-patterned *huipil* fabric in the Taylor Museum is unlike any woven in that community. The man's trousers bear the stamp of the factory at Cantel where the fabric was milled. The woolen jackets and aprons are local treadle-loomed products (Figure 57).

EL QUICHÉ Zacualpa

Pueblo Viejo or "old town," as the name Zacualpa translates, indeed occupies the ruins of at least two Precolumbian towns. El Cementerio and Zacualpa are sites within about two miles of each other on a steep-sided plateau. Both were settled during the Postclassic period (900-1524 A.D.) by the Quiché ancestors of the present-day population, who continue to use an area of the ancient town as a cemetery. The red-striped rectangular shawl (Taylor Museum 776) is woven on the backstrap loom, as is the requisite triangular head covering which is part of the village costume.

Figure 59. Huipil from Aguacatán, ca. 1970. Gordon Frost Collection.

Figure 37. *Huipil* from Mixco, ca. 1900. Lowie 3-239.

Figure 56. Man's costume from Santo Tomás Chichicastenango, ca. 1930. Jacket: TM 1008, Trousers: TM 1009, Sash: TM 1010, *Tzute:* TM 1006, Blanket: TM 616.

Figure 53. *Huipil* fabric from San Pedro Ayampuc, ca. 1930. TM 763.

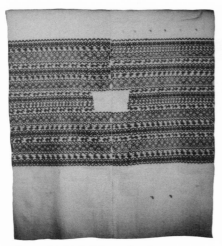

Figure 39. *Huipil* from San Juan Sacatepéquez, ca. 1900. Lowie 3-242.

Figure 46. *Huipil* from San Pedro Chuarrancho, ca. 1930. TM 744.

Figure 47. *Cofradía huipil* from San Pedro Ayampuc, ca. 1930. TM 769.

Figure 45. Detail of *huipil* from San Pedro Sacatepéquez, ca. 1970. Gordon Frost Collection.

Figure 48. Huipil fabric from San Pedro Sacatepéquez, ca. 1930. TM 824.

Figure 17. Huipil fabric from San Juan Comalapa, ca. 1970. Gordon Frost Collection.

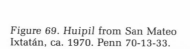

Figure 69. Huipil from San Mateo Ixtatán, ca. 1970. Penn 70-13-33.

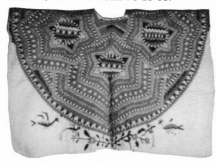

Figure 66. Huipil and shawl from Jacaltenango, ca. 1930. *Huipil:* TM 803, Shawl: TM 805.

Figure 29. Huipil from Tecpán, ca. 1970. Gordon Frost Collection.

Figure 19. Huipil from San José Poaquil, ca. 1930. TM 767.

Santa Cruz del Quiché, Sacapulas, Joyabaj, San Juan Cotzal, Aguacatán

Figure 57. Man's costume from Chiché, ca. 1930. Shirt: TM 620, Jacket: TM 1026, Trousers: TM 1024, Apron: TM 1023.

EL QUICHÉ, HUEHUETENANGO

Shared weaving styles among these communities represent social linkages that crosscut linguistic and political boundaries. Since Precolumbian times, trade networks have been maintained in order to ensure the exchange of goods between different, ecologically specialized regions.

The Quiché town of Sacapulas and the mixed Quiché and Aguacatec-speaking town of Aguacatán are situated in the semi-tropical valley of the Rio Negro. From these towns come a wide variety of warm-climate agricultural products (the name Aguacatán translates as "place of many avocados"), fish, and copper.

Salt was one of the most highly prized and essential trade commodities during Precolumbian times. Sacapulas is still a major salt-making center. The strategic location of Sacapulas, in combination with its resources, has made it a crossroads for trade between the high-country zones of Ixil speakers to the north in the Cuchumatanes mountains (including the village of San Juan Cotzal) and the central Quiché area to the south, surrounding the departmental capital of Santa Cruz del Quiché and the ancient Quiché capital of Utatlán. The mountain community of Joyabaj lies along the ancient trade route to central Mexico, home of the Aztec empire at the time of the conquest. It is thus probable that the Joyabaj area became a liaison between the regional trade network described above and interregional trade to Mexico.

For everyday wear, Sacapulas, Aguacatán, and Joyabaj women don a short, white single-panel *huipil* which hangs loose to the top of the skirt. At the turn of the century the only decoration on these *huipiles* consisted of red "sun pattern" appliqué or embroidery around the neckline, and perhaps a hand-scalloped bottom edge (Figure 58). By the 1930s, when the sewing machine had made its way into community workshops, tightly standardized birds and flowering vines began to be machine stitched across the backs of the *huipiles*. Machine-stitched tucks in horizontal bands and floral embroidery on necklines also appeared around this time. On *huipiles* in collections made after 1950, these decorative features are more elaborate. Commercial lace or eyelet often replaces the handstitched border scallops, and machine-embroidered ribbons embellish the newer garments. Another recent change in some *huipiles* is the use of commercial floral-patterned damask cloth for ground fabric (Figure 59). Although commercial cloth has long been used for *huipiles*, the women continue to weave their blue skirts on the backstrap loom.

The more typical daily *huipil* style of Joyabaj, with its embroidered floral decoration, exhibits definite Mexican influence (Figure 60). Today, in response to the increasing availability of shiny cotton embroidery thread (*lustrina*) in a variety of colors, the design area is worked mainly in acrylics instead of silk, and has expanded to encompass most of the garment. The motifs and their arrangement, however, have changed very little (Figure 61). The striped ground fabric has been either predominantly blue or red since at least 1930. Assuming that the provenance for a *huipil* (ca. 1930) in the University Museum of the University of Pennsylvania is correct, this style was also worn in Sacapulas.

The ceremonial *huipil* of Sacapulas, represented in collections dating between 1920 and 1975 — with three-panel construction, four-scalloped appliqué pattern around the neckline, and a mainly red banding pattern (Figure 62) — resembles the daily *huipil* of northern Ixil-speaking neighbors in cut and layout of design. The Ixil are represented in the Taylor Museum collection by a *huipil* from the village of San Juan Cotzal (Figure 63). Patterning on *huipiles* of this village is no longer predominantly red, but blue and green with accents of turquoise, red, pink, and purple (Figure 64).

An anomalous *huipil* style from Sacapulas, dating to the turn of the century, is shown in Figure 65. An identical *huipil* from San Pedro Jocopilas (El Quiché) is in the University of Pennsylvania collection. The latter village, on the route between Santa Cruz del Quiché and Sacapulas, has used only a commercially made blouse, like that worn in Santa Cruz del Quiché, since at least 1930. The origin, distribution, and disappearance of the older-style *huipil* presents an interesting problem for future study.

Figure 61. Huipil from Joyabaj, ca. 1970. UCLA X76-1196, gift of Caroline and Howard West.

HUEHUETENANGO Chiantla

The Mam-speaking municipality of Chiantla, with a population of over 15,000 people, encompasses high mountains rising from the outskirts of the town center, deep river valleys, and canyons. The pine-forested mountains are rich in lead and other minerals. Along with temperate and cold-zone crops of wheat and potatoes, the people of Chiantla raise cattle and sheep whose wool is spun and woven locally or traded in regional marketplaces. The skirt in the Taylor Museum collection (TM 653) is of solid- and *ikat*-striped cotton.

HUEHUETENANGO Jacaltenango

Jacaltenango ("house of water") is populated mainly by Jacaltec-speaking Maya and is one of the largest towns in this department. Until 1975, when a road was paved into the town through the Cuchumatanes mountains from Huehuetenango, Jacaltenango remained relatively isolated. The striped, plain weave textiles represented in the Taylor Museum collection are rarely made today. Such backstrap weaving has been supplanted by commercially milled cloth.

The Jacaltenango *huipil* in the Taylor Museum (Figure 66) is typical of those woven in this town to the present day. The raised spots of color are created on the front of the fabric by wrapping and knotting pattern wefts around warp threads. A definite Spanish influence is evident in the large ruffled collar found on all *huipiles*. Machine-stitched tucks in the collar at the neckline are today the specialty of a few enterprising townswomen. Although only this *huipil* style was represented in the collections studied, Anderson, in her study of contemporary Guatemalan textiles, notes that several new types are worn by the younger generation (Anderson 1978:185).

Figure 65. Huipil from Sacapulas, ca. 1900. AMNH 65/2128.

San Mateo Ixtatán

Figure 67. *Huipil* from San Mateo Ixtatán, ca. 1900. Penn 29-60-1.

Figure 68. *Huipil* from San Mateo Ixtatán, ca. 1930. TM 713.

San Miguel Acatán

HUEHUETENANGO

San Mateo Ixtatán is a remote Chuj-speaking community in the northwest corner of the Guatemalan Highlands. The view north from the high country of the municipality, which is situated at an elevation of about 8,580 feet, is of magnificent jagged mountains and steep canyons sloping to an altitude of around 990 feet at the border with Chiapas, Mexico. Four pure saltwater springs owned and worked communally by the townspeople bubble up through the limestone and volcanic rock. In addition to salt making and small-scale farming, the Chuj of San Mateo Ixtatán weave palm-leaf mats and hats.

The typical *huipil* of Ixtatán is composed of two to four layers of commercial muslin and decorated boldly with satin stitch embroidery. Hanging loosely, almost to the knees, this *huipil* is reminiscent of its Precolumbian antecedents. Another unusual feature is the pattern-cut of the cloth. Two pieces of fabric are first pinned at the sides to form a tubular body. Then, another piece of cloth is folded along its length and a neckhole is cut in its center. Finally, it is joined to the top of the tube to create a top yoke.

The development of this *huipil* style in the twentieth century is clearly documented in the textile collections studied. Prior to 1910, the concentric pattern surrounding the neckline, mainly in red with accents of yellow, green, or magenta, was relatively small and had a collarlike effect. Below this "collar" was a red band of satin stitching covering the yoke seam (Figure 67). During the 1930s and 1940s, more collars were added to the dominant red scheme and the collar pattern surface became enlarged so that the red yoke-band was intersected or eliminated altogether (Figure 68). The culmination of this stylistic trend in the modern period (1950-1975) is shown (Figure 69). The modern sunburst design not only vibrates with color, combining as many as seven or eight colors in a single piece, but is more complex in pattern. Optical effects created by, for example, alternating dark- and light-colored slopes of a zigzag motif that give an impression of three dimensionality, are well represented in the collections.

HUEHUETENANGO

The Chuj community of San Miguel Acatán encompasses the valleys, foothills, and high mountains of the Cuchumatanes range. In the cool, high altitudes, as elsewhere in the region, men wear a locally made dark woolen tunic called a *capixay*. The particular style worn in Acatán is fringed at the bottom edge and hangs almost to the knees. The woman's red wraparound skirt (Taylor Museum 806) is worn with a *huipil* of the same color and a necklace of glass beads or silver coins.

HUEHUETENANGO San Pedro Necta

Some of the steepest mountains of the Cuchumatanes range surround the town center of the San Pedro Necta municipality. In the plaza a colonial church still stands. Speakers of the Mam language, the people of San Pedro Necta grow sugar cane and bananas in the warm, fertile valleys of the Selegua and Santa Ana Huista rivers. From the forested mountain slopes they obtain pine, cedar, and other woods. Principal industries include the production of woolen cloth and clay tiles.

Although some men still wear the woolen tunic, or *capixay*, held in place with a wide red cotton sash, it is the women who maintain the most traditional costumes, as is the case in most towns. The women's *huipil* hangs loose to the hips and is distinctive in its pattern-cut. A single length of fabric is doubled and seamed along the side and at the top of the shoulders with an opening left for the head. The Taylor Museum *huipil* (Figure 70) is a very simplified type donned for hard work. The *huipil* depicted in Figure 71 is more typical of the daily *huipil* style. Its decoration is noteworthy for the combination of horizontal ground fabric stripes with vertically arranged brocaded motifs, whereas the reverse arrangement is far more common, i.e. vertical ground fabric stripes with horizontally arranged brocaded motifs. Motifs of simple linear geometrics — similar to those used in neighboring towns of Santiago Chimaltenango, San Rafael Petzal, Colotenango, and San Miguel Ixtahuacán — are done in a supplementary weft wrapping technique that imparts to them a raised texture.

San Pedro Necta women have not, as in so many towns, abandoned the practice of weaving their own skirts on the backstrap loom. The San Pedro men's and women's custom of tying the red sash around their waists, so that the ends hang loose in back like tails, is unique.

Figure 70. Work *huipil* from San Pedro Necta, ca. 1930. TM 804.

Figure 72. Woman's costume from Santiago Chimaltenango, ca. 1930. Blouse: TM 1021, Skirt: TM 1020, Sash: TM 1022, Headband: TM 1057.

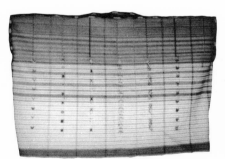

Figure 71. *Huipil* from San Pedro Necta, ca. 1970. UCLA X75-804, gift of Caroline and Howard West.

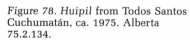

Figure 78. *Huipil* from Todos Santos Cuchumatán, ca. 1975. Alberta 75.2.134.

Figure 82. *Huipil* from Almolonga, ca. 1970. UCLA X76-1140, gift of Caroline and Howard West.

Figure 84. Men's sashes from Concepción Chiquirichapa, ca. 1930. TM 729 for Good Friday, 732, and 733.

Figure 87. *Huipil* from San Martín Sacatepéquez, ca. 1970. UCLA X76-1139, gift of Caroline and Howard West.

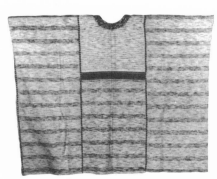

Figure 88. *Cofradía huipil* from Quezaltenango, ca. 1930. TM 674.

Figure 92. *Cofradía huipil* from Quezaltenango, ca. 1930. MARI G.17.4, 41-50 A.

Figure 93. *Huipil* from Quezaltenango, ca. 1930. MARI G.17.4, 42-48.

Figure 94. Daily *huipil* from Quezaltenango, ca. 1970. UCLA X75-812, gift of Caroline and Howard West.

Figure 95. Huipil from Olintepeque, ca. 1930. TM 665.

Figure 96. Huipil from Olintepeque, ca. 1970. Heard NA-CA-Gu-C-200.

Figure 98. Huipil from Zunil, ca. 1900. AMNH 63/3496.

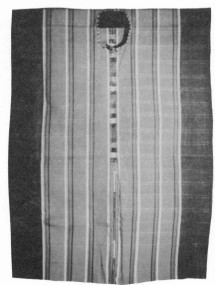

Figure 100. Huipil from Zunil, ca. 1970. Penn 70-13-70a.

Figure 102. Servilleta from San Antonio Aguas Calientes, ca. 1930. TM 609.

Santiago Chimaltenango

Figure 73. Man's costume from Santiago Chimaltenango, ca. 1930. *Tzute:* TM 725, *Sash:* TM 726, *Capixay:* TM 728.

Santa Eulalia

San Rafael Petzal

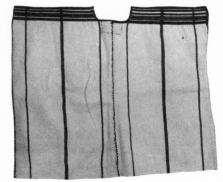

Figure 74. *Huipil* from San Rafael Petzal, ca. 1930. TM 706.

HUEHUETENANGO

About half an hour's drive from San Pedro Necta, over an exceedingly rough road, lies the village of Santiago Chimaltenango. The people of this town speak Mam. In recent years, the establishment of a weaving cooperative in town has provided an impetus for traditional weaving and has encouraged some stylistic changes as well. For instance, the cooperative has encouraged the production of *huipiles* with different background colors than the red used by townswomen for distribution to outside communities (Anderson 1978:88).

With its puffed, set-in sleeves, the *huipil* of Santiago Chimaltenango is more accurately described as a blouse. The small, linear geometric motifs brocaded in a wrap technique are like those of other towns in the region — San Pedro Necta, San Rafael Petzal, and San Ildefonso Ixtahuacán. In all of these villages women wear a similar long woolen headband wrapped halo-fashion around the crown of the head. The dark blue skirt is still woven by the women on their backstrap looms (Figure 72). Despite the isolation of the town, the men have virtually abandoned the traditional garments such as those represented in the Taylor Museum (Figure 73).

HUEHUETENANGO

Situated high in the Cuchumatanes mountains, Santa Eulalia has a year-round cold climate. Nonetheless, cereal grains are cultivated and wood is plentiful in the surrounding forests. The principal industry of the town is wool weaving done by men on the treadle loom, while the women weave their *huipiles* and belts on the backstrap loom. Although not present in the Taylor Museum's piece (TM 807), it is not uncommon for the women's long skirts to have wool woven into their basically cotton fabric. The Santa Eulalia *huipil* is long and white with colorful floral embroidery around the neckline.

HUEHUETENANGO

In the native Mam language the word *petzal* means "heavy tortoise." The town center is nestled in the temperate foothills of the Cuchumatanes mountains near the banks of the Selegua River. Until 1890, San Rafael Petzal was part of the neighboring municipality of Colotenango and was again annexed to Colotenango in 1935. It did not regain its independence as a municipality until 1947. The similarities are therefore not surprising between costumes of San Rafael Petzal, Colotenango, and Ixtahuacán, also once part of Colotenango. Of the women's garments, the principally red- and yellow-striped skirt with vertical rows of small embroidered motifs has remained virtually identical among the three towns, although the *huipiles* have become more stylistically diverse.

Documented in the collections are three types of *huipil* from this community. The Taylor Museum *huipil* (Figure 74) made up of two panels of cotton fabric, is the earliest of those studied and the most simple in design. It is probably a work *huipil* or that of a poor woman. The typical *huipil* style represented in modern (post-1960) collections has a red- and white-striped ground fabric, three-panel construction, and is considered to be among the most magnificent supplementary weft designs in the Highlands (Figure 75). Especially noteworthy is the sophisticated way in which colors are combined and recombined using the same simple motifs, thus adding interest and variety without sacrificing harmony of the design as a whole. Each motif unit is a beautiful exercise in the aesthetics of color. The many permutations of color among these units are reminiscent of our modern computer-derived designs. San Rafael Petzal weavers also create the optical effects of movement and transparency in *huipil* motifs by overlapping motifs and colors. Another *huipil* style that was found in several modern collections has a plain white ground. With the exception of the *pecho* ("breast band") in typical San Rafael Petzal motifs, it resembles the *huipil* of Ixtahuacán quite closely (Figure 76).

Figure 76. Huipil from San Rafael Petzal, ca. 1970. Gordon Frost Collection.

HUEHUETENANGO

Todos Santos Cuchumatán

About twenty-five miles from the departmental capital of Huehuetenango, Todos Santos occupies rugged terrain in the Cuchumatanes foothills. In this cool region, men herd sheep, spin, and weave wool on treadle looms. The women are potters and cotton textile weavers who produce all of their clothing except for their skirts, which are traded in from the foot loom workshops of Huehuetenango. Called the granary of Huehuetenango, Todos Santos produces potatoes, maize, wheat, and cool-country fruits and vegetables, which are traded in regional marketplaces. Atop the four mountain peaks surrounding the town center are altars to different Maya deities where aboriginal ritual is still practiced.

In this town the men and women still use traditional costume even for daily wear. A Cuchumalteco is easily identified by his red- and white-striped outfit with woolen overpants which appears fairly bizarre to an outsider. Leather sandals with a heel cup typical of the Cuchumatán region are worn by both men and women, as are distinctive square-crowned hats of plaited palm leaf. Osborne (1965:191) reports that men of wealth are distinguished by a third hatband added to the customary two.

Changes in the *huipil* style over the past eighty years are documented in the collections. A general trend toward more elaborate decoration has been identified with an increase in the amount of brocading, often covering most of the ground fabric, and in the number of design motifs and colors used in a single piece. This trend is paralleled in design on men's cotton pants and shirts. From the early 1900s until the post-1940s, Todos Santos *huipiles* were mainly red and white with accents of yellow, green and/or blue. The only design motifs were stripes and blocks of color (Figure 77). While this style is still used, more prevalent are *huipiles* that have additional design motifs of stepped diamonds, chevrons, and several types of zigzags, as well as new colors such as turquoise and magenta (Figure 78). Another change is a decrease in the prominence of the cloth collar. The flounce collar, introduced by the Spaniards, has gradually become reintegrated into a native yoke. This is small, usually square, and firmly stitched down with rickrack — often in a colored fabric that blends into the overall color scheme (Figure 79).

Figure 79. Huipil from Todos Santos Cuchumatán, ca. 1970. Gordon Frost Collection.

Almolonga

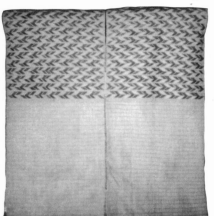

Figure 81. *Huipil* from Almolonga, ca. 1930. MARI G.17.6, 41-45 A.

QUEZALTENANGO

Almolonga is a mountain village about nine miles from Quezaltenango. Its name means "place where water springs" and was inspired by the many clearwater springs of the area. The people of Almolonga speak Quiché and are primarily occupied with the cultivation of vegetables and flowers that they market in Quezaltenango. For a short time during the sixteenth century, Almolonga was the seat of the Spanish colonial government. The town was extensively damaged by a flood and earthquake in 1541 and the capital was moved to Antigua.

The richly brocaded textiles of Almolonga dazzle the eye with their repetitive parallelogram or zigzag patterning and systematic alternation of colors. Women continue to wear their "traditional costume" but, in recent years, they have adopted the *huipiles* of Quezaltenango for daily use. The men no longer don their native dress except for ceremonial occasions.

Two styles of *huipil* are woven on the backstrap loom in Almolonga. The first, found in collections dating to the first half of the century but also described in contemporary literature (Pettersen 1976:46-47), features horizontal brocaded bands differentiated by motifs and color changes (Figure 80). The second style is characterized by two-dimensional pattern and the design is unrestricted by the band structure. In the earliest example of this style in the collections (Figure 81), the horizontal bands are still visible, although dominated by the overall pattern. In the contemporary *huipiles*, like the man's shirt of previous decades (Figure 80), the banding is omitted altogether (Figure 82). The red ginghamlike ground fabric is typical of *huipiles* and men's shirts, although a solid red ground is also used for men's shirts. Dark blue *ikat* stripes are also common in *huipiles*. For daily use, women wear a plain dark blue skirt tightly wrapped and tucked at the waist without the aid of a belt.

Concepción Chiquirichapa, San Juan Ostuncalco

Figure 83. *Servilleta* and women's headbands from Concepción Chiquirichapa, ca. 1930. *Servilleta*: TM 724, Headbands: TM 730, 731.

QUEZALTENANGO

These two communities are neighboring municipalities whose principal industry is the small-scale production of wicker baskets. San Juan Ostuncalco is a daughter community of Concepción Chiquirichapa and, although independent since the seventeenth century, their historical relationship is reflected in some of their weavings. For example, complex design motifs of fringed and serrate diamonds, long-tailed birds, and treelike or plantlike forms, as well as their interlocking arrangement on the ground fabric, appear in textiles from both communities.

Chiquirichapa and Ostuncalco share the same style of women's hairband (Figure 83). It is worn either crossing the top of the head from the left to tie the hair at the nape of the neck, or tied at the side of the head with the ends hanging loose to the shoulder. Ceremonial textiles woven of the precious native *cuyuscate* and brocaded in silk floss denote the high social status of the wearer. The *servilleta* in the Taylor Museum is an example (Figure 83). The tree of life motif decorating this *servilleta* is also prominent on ceremonial textiles of Quezaltenango; Osborne contends that it is derived from an ancient Mam symbol of high caste (1965:92).

The only vestige of men's traditional costume (*traje*) surviving since the middle of the century are the long backstrap-loomed sashes (Figure 84). These are

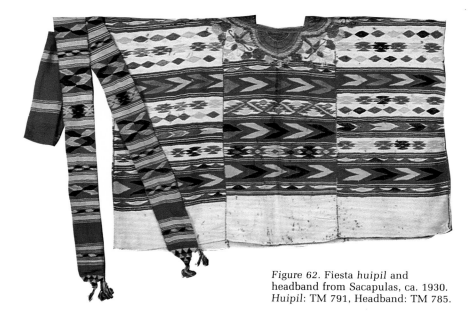

Figure 62. Fiesta *huipil* and headband from Sacapulas, ca. 1930. *Huipil:* TM 791, Headband: TM 785.

Figure 64. Huipil from San Juan Cotzal, ca. 1970. UCLA X76-1206, gift of Caroline and Howard West.

Figure 75. *Huipil* from San Rafael Petzal, ca. 1970. Gordon Frost Collection.

Figure 80. Man's and woman's clothing from Almolonga, ca. 1930. Fiesta *huipil*: TM 999, Fiesta skirt: TM 1000, Man's shirt: TM 699.

Figure 77. Man's and woman's costumes from Todos Santos Cuchumatán, ca. 1930. Woman's costume: *Huipil*: TM 1004, Sash: TM 1003, Skirt: TM 1005; Man's costume: Shirt: TM 709, Trousers: TM 710, Overtrousers: TM 704, Sash: TM 708, Kerchief: TM 707, Hat: TM 683.

Figure 86. Huipil from San Martín
Sacatepéquez, ca. 1970. Heard
NA-CA-Gu-C-67.

Figure 91. *Huipil* from
Quezaltenango, ca. 1930. TM 679.

Figure 118. Woman's costume from
Panajachel, ca. 1930. Fiesta *huipil*:
TM 640, Skirt: TM 637, Sash:
TM 629, Tzute: TM 633.

Figure 107. *Cofradía huipil* from
Santa María Cauque, ca. 1930.
TM 686.

purportedly markers of status and descent. One example in the Taylor Museum collection (TM 729) was documented in field notes made by Ricketson as being worn on Good Friday. The man's sash from Concepción Chiquirichapa in the Taylor Museum (TM 733) is similar to the work of San Martín Sacatepéquez (Chile Verde).

QUEZALTENANGO

San Martín Sacatepéquez (Chile Verde)

Figure 85. Woman's costume from San Martín Sacatepéquez, ca. 1930. Fiesta *huipil*: TM 735, Skirt: TM 736, Sash: TM 727.

Bordering Concepción Chiquirichapa on the southwest is another Mam municipality, San Martín Sacatepéquez. The inhabitants of this small community, which is better known as Chile Verde for the locally grown vegetable, are barely able to cultivate enough of the rugged rocky terrain to subsist. Compounding this problem is the fact that the most fertile slopes remain in the hands of *Ladino* or European coffee growers. However, volcanic ash deposited over the centuries by the volcanoes Siete Orejas ("seven ears") and Chicabal has enhanced the fertility of the soil in the municipality. A lake is situated in the crater of Chicabal where the people of San Martín and neighboring villages go to perform native rituals, including the sacrifice of animals to propitiate their ancient deities.

As already noted, some aspects of Chile Verde weaving, particularly the types of design motifs and their pattern of arrangement, resemble that of the related peoples of Concepción Chiquirichapa and San Juan Ostuncalco. However, traditional costume or *traje* of Chile Verde, still worn by both men and women, is so finely woven and so spectacular in its distinctive design, that it deserves separate mention. Today, more backstrap weaving is done here than in the other two towns. The intricate patterns are brocaded with the fingers and without the aid of a pattern-stick tool. Instead of rewarping the loom for each of the two *huipil* panels, as is the usual practice, San Martín artisans weave the patterns for both panels in a single length, turning the loom around to begin the second panel design from the opposite end (Anderson 1978:123).

Huipiles of the period 1930-1950, like the example in the Taylor Museum collection (Figure 85), are typically patterned in mirrored horizontal bands of simple bold geometrics such as zigzags, diamonds, and chevrons. The motifs, in turn, are often constructed of tiny block or dot units giving a jewellike effect to the garment. Gold, light bluish green, and purple on a red ground are characteristic colors.

In contrast, the design on contemporary *huipiles* (those from the collections dating between 1960 and 1975) is not structured in bands, but exhibits a two-dimensional arrangement of motifs with almost no ground fabric showing between them. As many as six new colors, often of cotton *lustrina* rather than silk, can be found in a single garment.

Also documented in modern collections are two substyles: one using predominantly geometric motifs (Figure 86), and the other decorated with highly stylized bird and tree motifs similar to those found on some *huipiles* from Quezaltenango, *servilletas* from Concepción Chiquirichapa, and *fajas* ("men's sashes") from San Juan Ostuncalco (Figure 87). The woman's belt and hairband are the same as those worn in the latter two villages. In San Martín, however, the belt doubles as a swaddling cloth for newborn infants. The dark blue skirt is treadle loomed in San Juan Ostuncalco, although *ikat*-striped material from Quezaltenango may also be used.

Quezaltenango

Figure 89. Mass *huipil* from Quezaltenango, ca. 1930. TM 675.

Figure 90. *Cofradía huipil* from Quezaltenango, ca. 1930. MARI G.17.7, 41-51 A.

QUEZALTENANGO

The third largest city in Guatemala and the political and economic center of an extensive plateau region, Quezaltenango has a mixed *Ladino* and Maya population of over 40,000. Of the Maya people, most are Quiché and the remainder are Mam speakers. Originally a Mam center, the Precolumbian predecessor of Quezaltenango was taken over and colonized by the Quiché in the fifteenth century. The Quiché called their city Xelaju which, until the Spanish conquest in 1524, was the principal elite center of the region. The ancient site of Xelaju, believed to be located in the mountains surrounding the present-day city of Quezaltenango, has never been discovered. The city was renamed Quezaltenango ("place of the quetzal") by Alvarado's Mexican mercenaries. Situated on the northern slope of an active volcano, Quezaltenango was almost entirely rebuilt following a disastrous volcanic eruption in 1902. The city's factories produce and export throughout the Highlands a wide variety of commodities, including foot-loomed textiles for *huipiles,* skirts, and other garments.

No less that five distinct *huipil* styles, all of which are woven on treadle looms, have been made in Quezaltenango since at least the turn of the century. The two ceremonial styles, exemplified by the Taylor Museum pieces in Figures 88 and 89, are draped loosely over the top of a daily *huipil*. During processions they are worn over the head with the face encircled by the floral-embroidered neck opening, as is also done in the departments of Alta and Baja Verapaz. The *cofradía huipil* may either be brocaded solely in white cotton or may include gold and purple silk (Figure 90). Typical motifs for this type of *huipil* are a highly stylized ducklike bird atop a tree or corn plant, a type of rosette, a horselike creature, and human figures depicted hand-in-hand across the width of each fabric panel. The panels are joined with a simple silk *randa* ("figure-eight stitch") on an elaborate floral lattice.

The three *huipil* styles for daily use are characterized as follows: (1) with horizontal bands of *ikat* designs, alone or including bands of geometric brocaded designs (Figure 91); (2) with overall patterning of brocaded bird and tree motifs in purple and gold, different from those found on the *cofradía huipil* (Figure 92) and more closely paralleled by a style of *huipil* woven in recent years in San Martín Sacatepéquez (Figure 87); (3) with adjacent horizontal bands of elaborate diamond and zigzag motifs, usually in red or dark blue with accents of other colors (Figure 93). The first and second styles are represented in the collections from the pre-1930s and are made of two, rather than the three panels typical of later pieces. In addition, the design area is greatly reduced. Thus, when tucked into the skirt in the customary manner, the white ground fabric of these older pieces would have been visible above the waistband. A relatively recent change in some daily *huipiles* is the embroidery of large, European-style roses and other flowers at the neckline and down the panel seams (Figure 94).

A common statement in the literature is that Quezaltenango Indians are divided into as many as five distinct classes and that each has its own style of *huipil* with appropriate symbols (Osborne 1965:106, Pettersen 1976:118). According to Osborne, the second style described above (Figure 92) is known as *pishquin* and is associated with the high-caste Indians. Scantily patterned treadle-loomed *huipiles* characterize the lower class, while similar, but more elaborate *huipiles* with silk supplementary wefts are worn by women of the middle class. These are usually woven on the backstrap loom. From the descriptions given, these types cannot be positively matched with the styles found in the collections. Only in the University of Pennsylvania's Osborne collection (ca. 1930-1940) were *huipiles* designated by class affiliation. These data suggest that variations within the styles described above may be at least as important with respect to social status as the fact of different styles themselves.

QUEZALTENANGO Olintepeque

Olintepeque is a Quiché town situated about 4⅓ miles from Quezaltenango, in a small valley in an arm of the Andean cordillera. Olintepeque translates as "in the mountains which tremble."

Two types of *huipil* are worn in Olintepeque. One is made of three panels and features a red- and white-striped ground fabric with wider bands of red on the center panel than on the sides (Figure 95). The other style is made of two widths and has horizontal dark blue and magenta bands sometimes bordered by thin white stripes (Figure 96). Common in samples dating to the post-1940 period are black velvet bindings and, in the red and white style, pleats at either side of the center panel. The latter feature is also found in modern *huipiles* from Quezaltenango. Both *huipil* styles, as well as the woman's ankle-length wraparound skirt, are treadle loomed. The *ikat*-striped skirt material of Quezaltenango is also used here, but is wrapped and gathered at the front in the customary style of this municipality.

QUEZALTENANGO Zunil

The town of Zunil is situated in a fertile basin surrounded by mineral-rich mountains and canyons. The nearby volcano, which shares the name of the municipality, heats steaming thermal springs at which the Indians gather to bathe. Approximately six miles from the town center, on a mountain shelf overlooking the Samala River, lies the preconquest Quiché site of Chuitinamit. Its location, directly above a major pass connecting the Highlands to the Piedmont, attests to the antiquity of this modern-day interregional trade route.

In Zunil, the characteristic *huipil* and the man's shirt of the 1930s-1940s (Figure 97) are similarly patterned in vertical purple plain weave stripes, sometimes accented by orange, green, or yellow stripes. The *huipil*, left unseamed under the arms and tucked into a knee-length wraparound skirt, has undergone some dramatic changes over the past eighty years. For example, a brocaded *huipil* in the collection of the American Museum of Natural History dating to the early decades of this century (Figure 98) contrasts strongly in style with that described above. Because this is the only example from the early period in the collections studied, it is not possible to determine whether it is typical or not. A more recent change in *huipil* styles is, however, clearly documented in the collections. In contemporary pieces (ca. 1960-1975), the bluish white foundation (created by a white weft and blue warp) has been displaced in favor of a broadly-striped central area, boldly colored in bright red, magenta, yellow, or green and accented by thinner stripes and a *randa* ("figure-

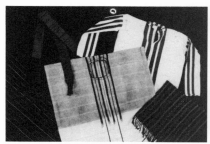

Figure 97. Man's and woman's costumes from Zunil, ca. 1930. *Huipil*: TM 681, Shawl: TM 682, Woman's sash: TM 685, Woman's *servilleta*: TM 678, Man's shirt: TM 832.

eight stitch") in contrasting colors (Figures 99, 100). Anderson (1978:74) also reports that some contemporary Zunil *huipiles* have thin black and white stripes bordering the central design area. The practice of isolating a central area by color contrast gives the illusion of three-panel breadths to these two-breadth *huipiles*. It was not possible to determine whether a parallel stylistic change has occurred in the men's shirts.

Magdalena Milpas Altas

Figure 101. Woman's costume from Magdalena Milpas Altas, ca. 1930. *Huipil*: TM 719, Fiesta *tzute*: TM 721, Sash: TM 723.

San Antonio Aguas Calientes

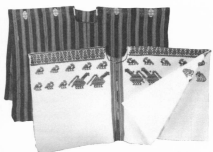

Figure 108. *Cofradía huipil* and daily *huipil* from Santo Domingo Xenacoj, ca. 1930. *Cofradía huipil*: TM 739, Daily *huipil*: TM 818.

SACATEPÉQUEZ

The Spanish name Milpas Altas means "high fields" and appropriately describes this municipality. Its town center is located on one of several high mountains of the area. Springs of clear, potable water flow from three other peaks: Monterrico, Las Minas, and El Carmen. The Cakchiquel people of Milpas Altas celebrate the day of their patron saint, Mary Magdalene, on July 22.

The women and girls of this community usually wear their *huipil* over a store-bought cotton blouse, allowing the sleeves and the neck of the undergarment to show. In its horizontal banding pattern, lightning motifs, and limited use of color, the Taylor Museum *huipil* of Milpas Altas (Figure 101) resembles the daily *huipil* from the same period of its neighbor to the east, Mixco. The *tzute* is customarily folded on the diagonal and tied at the hip, while the belt is wound tightly around the waist and secured with the pompons at the back. Osborne notes that the most beautifully decorated *tzutes* are restricted in their use to married women (1965:76).

SACATEPÉQUEZ

A few miles from the departmental capital of Antigua, Aguas Calientes is one of five settlements that surrounded Lake Quilisamapa until it was drained in 1928. The name Aguas Calientes or "hot waters," was derived from this body of water. Local tradition states that shortly after the conquest the Spaniards moved the townspeople from their homes located in the surrounding hills and founded the present-day town in the open valley (Lathbury 1974:15). In the seventeenth century, the people of Aguas Calientes joined together to purchase the land from their Spanish overlords. Periodically fertilized by ash from the nearby Volcan Fuego ("fire volcano"), the land is still farmed communally. The women of San Antonio are among the most prolific and skilled of all Guatemalan backstrap weavers. Almost all of the townswomen are weavers and produce textiles for local, regional, and even international markets. Tourist shops of textile vendors are a common site in San Antonio and Antigua.

The small *servilleta* in the Taylor Museum (Figure 102) documents the relatively early influence of the tourist market on weaving motifs. Deer, dogs, and men on bicycles, such as those that adorn this piece, as well as flower and fruit motifs from store-bought pattern books, are today common subjects in San Antonio weaving, although more traditional geometric patterns are also used. Several different styles of *servilleta* from the same period (ca. 1930-1945) are represented in the collections. One piece features rainbow-colored horizontal bands and *ikat* (*jaspe*) patterning (Figure 103). Others have either white or dark blue ground color and incorporate three groups of vertical striping at the center and edge, crosscut by small brocaded motifs. Woven into the fabric of another *servilleta* are the words "Es un recuerdo de la Rosalie Lopez Octubre de 44" or "(This) is a souvenir of Rosalie Lopez October 1944."

SACATEPÉQUEZ

Santa María Cauque

Santa María Cauque is a hamlet of the municipality of Santiago Sacatepéquez, whose town center lies about 2½ miles distant. Despite its affiliation with Santiago Sacatepéquez, the costume of this settlement is quite different. Several types of *huipil* are represented in the Taylor Museum collection. The daily *huipil* (Figure 104) with a striped ground fabric of red and white and alternating rows of unique geometric motifs (Figure 105), is virtually identical to a contemporary *huipil* in the Heard Museum collection. Another *huipil* (Figure 106) designated as an "old style," differs in having a yellow checked ground fabric and small animal motifs in only two alternating colors. Animal motifs also decorate the three-panel *cofradía huipil* (Figure 107) which, in its design layout and in the motif units, resembles the *cofradía huipil* of San Pedro Sacatepéquez (Figure 51). It is virtually identical to one from Santo Domingo Xenacoj, suggesting stylistic diffusion between these weaving centers.

Figure 104. Huipil and sash from Santa María Cauque, ca. 1930. *Huipil*: TM 701, Sash: TM 698.

SACATEPÉQUEZ

Santo Domingo Xenacoj

In the local Cakchiquel language, the name Xenacoj means "we feel the pumas" and one can surmise that in times past these animals stalked the countryside around the town. Founded long before the conquest, Santo Domingo Xenacoj is bordered by the younger municipalities of San Juan Sacatepéquez on the northeast and by San Pedro Sacatepéquez on the east, with which it shares a well-established tradition of fine backstrap weaving and many stylistic elements.

Figure 105. Geometric motifs brocaded onto TM 701, *huipil* from Santa María Cauque.

The great deal of variability in *huipil* styles documented in the collections has resulted from combinations of stylistic elements unique to Xenacoj with others characteristic of San Juan and San Pedro Sacatepéquez in the department of Guatemala. For example, the Xenacoj double-headed bird on the *pechos* ("breast bands") of *cofradía huipiles* is distinctive. However, *huipiles* for daily use incorporate a vertically striped ground fabric, as in some types of *huipiles* from San Juan Sacatepéquez. Into several examples are incorporated large color-banded birds (Figure 108) which in modern pieces are often done in a rainbow-colored, picked-pile brocade such as that used in San Pedro Sacatepéquez. In Xenacoj, both *cofradía huipiles* (Figure 109) and daily *huipiles* bear humpbacked and long-necked birds with fretted appendages, commonly found on San Pedro *huipiles*. They also have the red and lavender color-banding of motifs typical of both San Juan and San Pedro. These features are documented in two very similar *cofradía huipiles* from Xenacoj dating to the turn of the century and to the post-1970 period, respectively. Finally, another type of Xenacoj ceremonial *huipil* in the University of Pennsylvania's collections is virtually identical to the *cofradía huipil* of Santa María Cauque, a nearby village in the same department (Figure 107). The processes of

Figure 109. *Cofradía huipil* from Santo Domingo Xenacoj, ca. 1900. AMNH 65/5892.

stylistic diffusion in the weaving of these communities deserve further investigation.

SACATEPÉQUEZ

Sumpango

Figure 110. Woman's costume from Sumpango, ca. 1930. *Huipil:* TM 991, Skirt: TM 990, Sash: TM 992, Hair tie: TM 1055.

Sumpango, or "hill of the belly," is a community of considerable antiquity, founded by the Cakchiquel long before the conquest. According to one source, the women of Sumpango have never been weavers and have relied upon the neighbors in Santo Domingo Xenacoj for all of their backstrap-woven goods (Pettersen 1976:170). Nevertheless, Sumpango women are expert embroiderers, the primary example of their work being the bright floral patterning around the neckline of their *huipiles.*

Typically, two *huipiles* are worn: one as an undergarment, tucked in, and the other not tucked into the skirt, and completely covering the *huipil* beneath. The undergarment is made of plain white, usually commercial cotton, and if decorated at all, has a colored *randa* ("figure-eight stitch") down the center seam or an overlay stitch around the neck opening. Top *huipiles,* from the 1930s and 1940s, as well as pieces from more modern periods, are vertically striped, mainly in red and natural brown cotton, like *huipiles* of Santo Domingo Xenacoj (Figure 110). There are accent stripes of yellow flanked by stripes of white or yellow in some 1930s-1940s examples, and by turquoise, green, or other bold colors in later pieces. This type of striped patterning is not found in Santo Domingo Xenacoj *huipiles.* Neckline embroidery consists of a ring of flower motifs pendant from a concentric pattern of triangles or scallops. Modern *huipiles* employ *lustrina* in an array of colors rather than the blue, green, and yellow silk floss of the earlier period. Because of the lower cost and greater availability of these threads, modern *huipiles* tend to be more heavily decorated with a greater variety of flower motifs. In addition to a larger floral "collar," there are rainbow-colored *randas* down the seams and overcast stitching around the neck and armholes. The Sumpango *huipil* in the Heard Museum collection (ca. 1970) represents a break with tradition, not only in this respect, but also in that it is made of commercial white cotton, formerly reserved for the undergarment. Should this represent a current trend, it would be interesting to learn how it affects, or was affected by, the commercial relationship with the weavers of Santo Domingo Xenacoj who purportedly have supplied the *huipil* fabric for Sumpango embroiderers.

The plain, dark blue skirt, like the *huipil,* exhibits more color in its *randa* embroidery today than in the 1930s-1940s period. Totonicapán supplies this town with hair ties which are coiled around the hair and then around the crown of the head.

San Marcos

SAN MARCOS

The city of San Marcos was founded by a group of Spaniards in Mam territory shortly after the conquest. At that time it held the status of a rural outpost under the jurisdiction of Quezaltenango. In 1752, at the instigation of some San Marcos townspeople, it was declared an independent municipality, although its independence continued to be disputed by Quezaltenango for many years. It was not until 1866 that the territory surrounding the town officially became the separate department of San Marcos with a capital of the same name. To this day, the city of San Marcos is sometimes referred to as San Marcos "El Barrio" ("the neighborhood"). This historical connection with Quezaltenango is clearly reflected in the weavings of San Marcos.

San Marcos *huipiles* of the 1930s and 1940s, such as the Taylor Museum example (Figure 111), share stylistic features with some types of Quezaltenango *huipiles* of the same period (Figure 93). Despite overlapping elements of color and brocaded patterning, the San Marcos *huipil* is woven on a backstrap, rather than a treadle loom. It is unique in its single-, rather than triple-breadth, design. The Taylor Museum *huipil* material (TM 651) is unusual in color scheme and treadle-loomed pattern, and may be a trade piece from Quezaltenango.

San Marcos *huipiles* of the 1960s and 1970s are of two breadths rather than the one found in the earlier period, and exhibit a far wider range of color combinations in their use of *lustrina* instead of silk in their brocaded designs. While some have retained the customary *mano* ("shoulder band") and bottom border and still appear to be backstrap loomed, others are made of treadle-loomed panels such as those made in Quezaltenango. Colorful *lustrina randas*, overcast-stitched necklines and armholes, and floral cotton collars adorn the modern examples. A Quezaltenango motif of long-tailed birds (*quetzales*) arranged in facing pairs is the primary brocaded motif on one modern *huipil* in the Heard Museum collection (NA-CA-Gu-C-27, not illustrated). In this example, traditional diamond shapes are used only as spaces between contiguous bands. A radical break with tradition in both color and patterning is exhibited by the University of Alberta *huipil* in Figure 112.

Figure 115. *Cofradía huipil* from Santa Catarina Nahualá, ca. 1970. Gordon Frost Collection.

SAN MARCOS   San Pedro Sacatepéquez

In 1876, President J. Rufino Barrios decreed that any Indian from this town who would, in the coming year, abandon native *traje* and adopt *Ladino* clothing would be officially recognized as having become a *Ladino*. This was conceived by Barrios as a means to "better" the lives of these Mam-speaking Maya, but most of them proudly maintain their native identity and textile traditions to this day. The predominance of yellow silk in the woman's costume is distinctive and San Pedro is the only town where the skirt fabric is loomed entirely of silk. The *refajo* ("skirt") (Figure 113) is often worn with an underskirt and an *ikat*-striped apron. In modern examples rayon is commonly substituted for the more costly silk threads.

SOLOLÁ   Santa Catarina Nahualá

The municipality of Nahualá is located about 18½ miles from the departmental capital of Sololá in the northwestern corner of the department. The name Nahualá is variously interpreted as "magic water," in reference to the nearby Nahuelate River, or as "place of the witches or magicians." Of Nahualá's approximately 20,000 inhabitants, the vast majority are Quiché Maya. These people are renowned for their traditionalism and pride in their ethnic heritage. They have a history of fierce

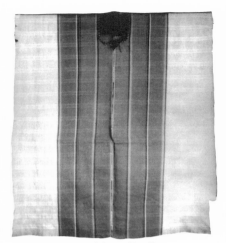

Figure 99. *Huipil* from Zunil, ca. 1970. Gordon Frost Collection.

Figure 103. *Servilleta* from San Antonio Aguas Calientes, ca. 1930. MARI G.14.3, 41-20 G.

Figure 119. *Huipil* from Panajachel, ca. 1975. Alberta 75.2.201.

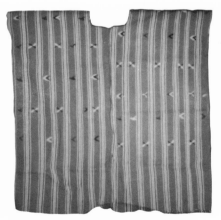

Figure 122. *Huipil* of a middle-class woman from San Andrés Semetabaj, ca. 1930. Penn 42-35-312.

Figure 126. *Huipil* from San Lucas Tolimán, ca. 1970. Gordon Frost Collection.

Figure 127. *Huipil* of an upper-class woman from San Lucas Tolimán, ca. 1930. Penn 42-35-315.

Figure 123. *Huipil* from San Andrés Semetabaj, ca. 1970. Gordon Frost Collection.

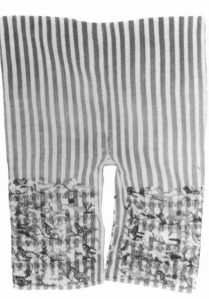

Figure 135. Man's trousers from Santiago Atitlán, ca. 1975. Alberta 75.2.114.

Figure 130. *Huipil* from San Marcos la Laguna, ca. 1930. TM 979.

Figure 133. *Huipil* from Santiago Atitlán, ca. 1970. Penn 70-13-89a.

Figure 120. Woman's costume from San Andrés Semetabaj, ca. 1930. *Huipil*: TM 981, Skirt fabric: TM 982, Sash: TM 980, *Servilleta*: TM 630, *Servilleta*: TM 632.

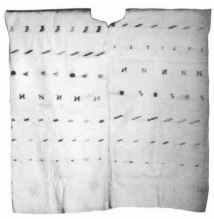

Figure 128. *Huipil* of a middle-class woman from San Lucas Tolimán, ca. 1930. Penn 42-35-316.

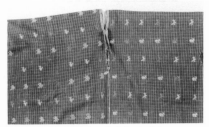

Figure 106. "Old style" *huipil* from Santa María Cauque, ca. 1930. TM 702.

Figure 116. Man's costume from Santa Catarina Nahualá, ca. 1930. Shirt: TM 985, Trousers: TM 989, Sash: TM 983, Neckerchief: TM 984, Apron: TM 986.

resistance to government attempts to impose a *Ladino* bureaucracy on the town and to turn over their lands to *Ladino* coffee growers. Despite their valiant efforts, however, a large portion of their ancestral farm land has become *Ladino*-owned coffee plantations.

The Quiché of Nahualá trace their descent to the Postclassic (900-1524 A.D.) town of Jija, the ruins of which are perched atop a volcanic mesa about twelve miles from Nahualá's town center. After the conquest the inhabitants were moved from this defensible site to the basin below, and the community of Santa Catarina Ixtahuacán was established. Nahualá, as an *aldea* ("hamlet") of Santa Catarina, declared its independence and became a separate municipality in the nineteenth century. Both communities, following an age old tradition, are the principal suppliers in Guatemala of local volcanic rock *manos* (grinding stones), and *metates* (grinding basins) (Fox 1978:156-157).

In Nahualá, native *traje* is still worn by men and women for both daily use and ceremonial occasions. Women's *huipiles,* such as Taylor Museum 658, may be plain white with only a brightly colored running stitch for decoration along the shoulder pleat and side seams. On others, especially those for special wear, the white ground fabric is divided into several densely brocaded areas with different motifs on front and back. On these pieces, design motifs of large birds with fretted appendages, lions and horselike creatures, and diamonds and zigzags are architecturally arranged in specific areas of the larger design field. For example, the Mass *huipil* in the Taylor Museum (Figure 114) illustrates the practice of highlighting a central horizontal band of diamond motifs. Narrower vertical bands of a geometric motif flank the sides. The preference is for predominantly red or lavender pattern wefts that bleed when washed and impart a pinkish tinge to the white ground fabric. Since the turn of the century, few changes in this conservative town's *huipil* style are documented in the collections other than the addition of several new colors such as turquoise, bright green, and orange and the substitution of rayon or cotton *lustrina* for silk floss. A modern three-panel *cofradía huipil* in the Gordon Frost collection is the only example of this style in all the collections. It features a large double-headed bird at the front center (Figure 115). Unlike the *huipil* for daily wear described above, the *cofradía huipil* is not tucked into the skirt. The woman's dark blue wrap skirt is usually worn falling to her heel and is twisted and rolled above the belt. The *randa* falls at hip level.

In the men's costume the only striking stylistic change documented in the collections is in the cotton shirt. In contrast to the white example with red brocaded cuffs and collar in the Taylor Museum collection (Figure 116), shirts of the past two decades are uniformly red- and yellow-striped with predominantly yellow-brocaded collar, cuffs, and pocket, as in the Heard Museum's example (Figure 117). The white pants are normally visible only in back, because the woolen kilt covers them in front.

Panajachel SOLOLÁ

Panajachel lies on the north shore of Lake Atitlán just below Sololá. Villagers from across the lake land their canoes here and unload produce for the marketplace in Sololá. In the local Cakchiquel language the name Panajachel means "place of the canes," which are abundant in the area. The ruins of an ancestral town of the

Postclassic period (900-1524 A.D.) called Ajchel, have yet to be located (Fox 1978:177).

The woman's costume of Panajachel in the Taylor Museum (Figure 118) includes two *huipil* varieties still seen today — that with mainly red cotton brocading and that adorned with purple silk floss. Although the former is classified as a fiesta *huipil*, both types are worn for daily use. Osborne claims that the more precious silk floss is reserved for married women and that single girls are allowed only cotton designs (1965:106). Along with these two *huipil* varieties is a new style illustrated in Figure 119. In this example, the striped ground fabric of the past has been replaced by solid red, brocaded in variegated strands of *lustrina* in bright shades of orange, blue, green, brown, and pink. Another modern *huipil* with purple *lustrina* decoration on a solid red ground also has a fringed back edge, despite the fact that the *huipiles* are customarily tucked into the tight wraparound skirt.

The *tzute* in the Taylor Museum is the type used to carry a baby or a package, or to drape a basket; it would not generally be worn on the head.

Figure 117. Man's shirt from Santa Catarina Nahualá, ca. 1970. Heard NA-CA-Gu-C-16.

SOLOLÁ San Andrés Semetabaj

San Andrés Semetabaj overlooks Lake Atitlán from a narrow mountain shelf at about 1,000 feet. The rugged topography surrounds the town center on three sides and makes flat arable land for subsistence or commercial cultivation scarce. In the 1960s, the Inter-American Highway was completed, connecting major commercial centers north of San Andrés and bypassing the town. Despite these geographic and strategic limitations, the Cakchiquel town of San Andrés has become a major producer of wheat, and in recent decades, a regional administrative center for a national association of agricultural cooperatives. On the local level, commerce is dominated by the women, who sell vegetables and backstrap-loomed textiles (Warren 1978:23-25).

The municipality has a population of approximately 3,500, about 1,000 of whom dwell in the town center. Of the latter, more than one-fourth are *Ladinos*, an unusually high proportion for this region. The biethnic character of this community as it is expressed in Indian mythology, ecology, religion, self-concept, and politics, is the subject of an excellent ethnographic study by Kay B. Warren entitled *The Symbolism of Subordination* (1978). Although the issues of stylistic change and symbolism in San Andrés weaving are not treated, the study provides a foundation for further research on these topics.

The *huipil* in the Taylor Museum collection (Figure 120) is much like that described by O'Neale (1945) as typical of San Andrés, and closely resembles a piece from the same period in the University of Pennsylvania collection. This is documented as an example of the style worn by noblewomen. Also in the University Museum collection are *huipiles* of the lowest class (Figure 121) and the middle class (Figure 122). San Andrés Semetabaj *huipiles* represented in ethnographic photographs and in collections dating to the post-1960s are examples of a particular stylistic variant of the lower-class *huipil* of preceding decades (Figure 123). These contemporary pieces differ mainly in their use of delicate individual motifs arranged in a dense overall pattern that covers most of the ground fabric. The bright green and

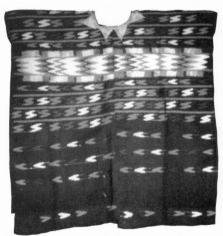

Figure 121. *Huipil* of a woman of the lowest class from San Andrés Semetabaj, ca. 1930. Penn 42-35-313.

blue *lustrina* and commercial neckline and armhole trims are also innovative. It is not known whether the *huipil* remains a marker of socioeconomic status in modern-day San Andrés Semetabaj, or whether such distinctions have their roots in preconquest society.

San Lucas Tolimán

Figure 125. Huipil from San Lucas Tolimán, ca. 1975. Alberta 75.2.234.

SOLOLÁ

San Lucas Tolimán is a mixed Cakchiquel- and Tzutujil-speaking community situated across the lake from Panajachel. Founded in the sixteenth century, its name is of Mexican origin and means "place where tule (a type of reed) is harvested."

A great deal of stylistic variability in *huipiles* is evident in the collections studied and in the descriptive literature. Because of its age, the Taylor Museum *huipil* (Figure 124) is somewhat unusual in its use of a colored rather than white foundation fabric, as well as in its brocaded color scheme. More typical of the pre-1940 period is a combination of red, yellow, and blue or green. In general, the Taylor Museum piece appears to be an early example of the style most prevalent in collections dating to the post-1960 period. In these pieces, such as in Figures 125 and 126, any of a number of brightly colored mercerized cottons may be used for the foundation fabric, and as many as ten may be incorporated into the brocaded pattern. More densely brocaded patterning, a square neckline trimmed with velvet or machine-embroidered ribbon, and sometimes pleats at either side of the center seam are all typical features of this style of modern *huipil*.

In the University of Pennsylvania collection, three different *huipil* styles are classified according to their association with the socioeconomic status of the wearer (Figures 127, 128). The *huipil* of the third, or lowest class, is a simple, unbrocaded type with red foundation striping like that of the upper-class style. A modern *huipil* in the Heard Museum and one in the Middle American Research Institute (ca. 1930-1940) most closely resemble the upper-class style, but have additional lightning-patterned *pechos* ("breast bands"). In still another variation in the Lowie Museum, the earliest of the *huipiles* studied (ca. 1900) combines the solid white foundation fabric of the middle-class example and the sun and moon appliquéd neckline of the upper-class *huipil*. It is, however, unique in having a red cloth *pecho* that reaches to within a few inches of either side seam (Figure 129).

San Marcos la Laguna, Santa Cruz la Laguna

SOLOLÁ

These two Cakchiquel municipalities are west of the departmental capital of Sololá. San Marcos is on the lakeshore while Santa Cruz reaches from the northern border of San Marcos into the cooler mountain region. Both specialize in the cultivation of grains and vegetables for subsistence and trade.

There were no textiles from these communities in the collections studied for comparison with the Taylor Museum pieces (Figure 130). O'Neale's descriptions of comparable pieces of roughly the same period (1945), suggest little stylistic variability with the exception of orange pinstripes on San Marcos *huipiles*, lacking in the Taylor Museum specimen. The Taylor Museum *tzute* from Santa Cruz is the type worn draped around a man's straw hat (O'Neale 1945:264).

SOLOLÁ Santa Lucía Utatlán

Santa Lucía Utatlán is situated in the cool and rugged mountain country above Lake Atitlán. A Quiché-speaking community, its namesake was the great Postclassic (900-1524 A.D.) capital of the Quiché nobility near the present town of Santa Cruz del Quiché, department of El Quiché. The most distinctive textiles of this municipality are *servilletas* of the type illustrated in Figure 131.

SOLOLÁ Santiago Atitlán

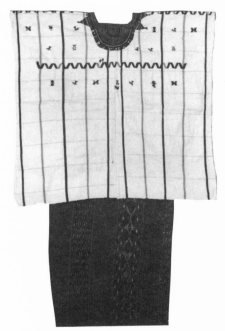

Santiago Atitlán is a Tzutujil-speaking community on the south shore of Lake Atitlán, with a population of more than 10,000. It lies up a long inlet in the shadow of the volcano Tolimán. There is a scarcity of arable land due to the rocky volcanic soil. However, the town's geographic location, at the juncture of the highlands to the northeast and west and the Pacific coastal lowlands to the south, makes trade between these regions a profitable means of subsistence. The men of Santiago Atitlán specialize in the transport of Highland produce (mostly vegetables), which they exchange for the rich variety of Lowland produce (such as tropical fruits and sugar cane). These are then sold in Highland markets around the lake and even in Chichicastenango. The dugout canoes (*cayucos*), used by all of the Lake Atitlán communities, are made in Santiago. Weaving remains an important activity for both men and women. *Jaspe* cloth for women's skirts and other garments is the principal product of treadle looms.

A woman of Santiago Atitlán is striking in her halolike headdress constructed of a narrow band of patterned red wool wound repeatedly around the crown of her head. In this village three types of *huipiles* are worn. The style represented in the Taylor Museum collection (Figure 132) is still seen today, but two new related types have become more common in recent decades. One, shown in Figure 133, employs a lavender and white vertically striped pattern crosscut by multicolored bands of brocaded zigzags. The zigzag motif has been used in this village since at least the 1930s. This is evidenced by the *pecho* of the *huipil* in the Peabody Museum (20/18259, not illustrated) dating to that period. However, the repetition of the single motif in a variety of brightly colored *lustrina* and acrylic yarns is a distinctly modern feature. The second modern *huipil* style (Figure 134) features bands of bird and flower motifs embroidered in free-form curvilinear patterns. These designs are of European origin, although neither their exact source, the means of introduction into the community, nor the process of stylistic change has been documented. A parallel stylistic change in men's shirts and trousers took place between the mid-1930s and the 1960s (Figure 135). The man's shirt in the Taylor Museum collection (Figure 136) is typical of the style observed in other contemporaneous collections. This same style is also found in collections dating to the post-1960 period. However, the lavender-and white-striped style made to be worn with the matching trousers shown in Figure 135 is more prevalent in these modern collections.

In both contemporary *huipil* styles, the traditional solar pattern appliquéd around the neckline is most often either replaced by, or entirely covered over with, floral embroidery. As the sun symbol was associated with Tojil, the important Precolumbian sky and war deity, the omission of the design or its relegation to a

Figure 132. Huipil and skirt from Santiago Atitlán, ca. 1930. Huipil: TM 1017, Skirt: TM 1016.

secondary pattern probably reflects changes in religious ideology, perhaps in the direction of a more orthodox Catholicism.

The predominantly red *ikat*-patterned skirt is wrapped tightly around the body and held in place without the aid of a sash simply by tucking and rolling the fabric at the waist. It is worn long — to the ankles — and, since at least 1930, has been produced with little or no apparent variation on local treadle looms.

Figure 131. *Servilleta* from Santa Lucía Utatlán, ca. 1930. TM 789.

Sololá   SOLOLÁ

Sololá, with a population of around 19,000, is the municipal capital of the department of Sololá. The town center, founded in 1547, is situated on the edge of a bluff overlooking Panajachel and Lake Atitlán. From the town, municipal lands extend northwest into the mountains where vegetable gardens and plots of wheat are etched into the terrain. These crops are the major source of cash income for the people of Sololá. On Fridays the town square is always lively with merchants and buyers from all of the lake communities, as well as from other areas of the Highlands.

The greatest amount of stylistic variability in Sololá weaving is found in the woman's *huipil*. There are two very different types made for daily and ceremonial use. The woman's top garment for daily wear with its set-in sleeves, is more accurately termed a blouse than a *huipil*, and is worn tucked into the skirt (Figure 137). The body of the blouse is made of four panels of *ikat*- and plain-striped fabric with separate pattern pieces for the sleeves and collar. The sleeves and collar may contrast in color with the body of the garment. For example, the body may be predominantly white with thin red stripes. Typical brocaded motifs include interlocking zigzags, blocks, and hourglass shapes placed singly on the upper back and upper front of the blouse. The major stylistic changes in this garment from the 1930s to the post-1960s consist of the use of broader stripes, which require less time and effort in warping the loom, along with a larger scale and range of color in the brocaded motifs (Figure 138).

The *cofradía* and Mass *huipil* styles (TM 635, Figure 137) differ in that the latter is three panels wide, is worn over the top of the skirt, and hangs almost to the knees.

The *cofradía* and Mass *huipil* styles (Taylor Museum 635, Figure 137) differ in that the latter is three panels wide, is worn over the top of the skirt, and hangs almost to the knees.

The Taylor Museum wedding *huipil* (Figure 137) typifies the style variously designated as "ceremonial," "Mass," "cofradía," or "wedding" that has been observed in other collections of the same period. In contrast, a ceremonial *huipil* in the Gordon Frost collection (Figure 139) provides a strikingly beautiful example of a stylistic innovation found alongside the older style in the post-1960 collections studied. The new style combines the color, *jaspe* banding, and the supplementary weft motifs of the woman's shirt for daily wear with the three-panel construction and sun-symbol-embroidered neckline of the traditional ceremonial *huipil*.

Figure 138. Blouse from Sololá, ca. 1970. UCLA X76-1156, gift of Caroline and Howard West.

TOTONICAPÁN   Momostenango

The name Momostenango means "at the wall every day" and refers to the frequent necessity during Precolumbian times to guard the town against attack. During the twentieth century, Momostenango has become the main center for the production and trade of wool weaving. Extremely rugged terrain and severe soil erosion force the townspeople to import much of their subsistence goods from the neighboring Quiché basin. The woolen industry provides a livelihood for many Momostenango families.

Many different styles of blanket are woven on treadle looms for home use, export to other Highland towns, or sale to tourists. A family usually specializes in one of the following styles: plaid, twill, *ikat*-patterned, striped, or checked commercially dyed souvenir blankets in bright colors. The process of making a blanket involves washing, carding, and spinning, usually performed by the men; weaving; and finally washing, soaking, and trampling the blanket in the local hot sulphur springs to produce a thick, fuzzy pile. Blankets and other weavings are sold at the Sunday market where materials are also purchased for the coming week's weaving. Although commercially spun and dyed yarns have become very popular, some weavers still prefer to purchase raw wool, preparing the yarns and dyeing with such natural substances as indigo (blue), brazilwood (deep purple), and cochineal (red).

Women use backstrap looms to weave skirts, *huipiles,* and utility cloths. Men working at their treadle looms produce blankets, woolen shawls, cotton and wool skirts, and men's woolen sashes such as the sash in the Taylor Museum collection (Figure 140). In contrast to the warp-striped Taylor Museum piece, a turn-of-the-century sash in the Lowie Museum is weft-striped in white, red, green, and yellow. O'Neale (1945) describes a Momostenango man's sash as warp-striped in white, black and red. The traditional male costume of Momostenango also includes white pants and a European-cut shirt of white muslin, over the top of which may be worn black woolen overpants similar to those worn in Todos Santos Cuchumatán (Figure 77).

Figure 140. Man's sash from Momostenango, ca. 1930. TM 756.

TOTONICAPÁN   San Cristóbal Totonicapán

San Cristóbal Totonicapán, or "hill of birds," is a Quiché-speaking community and a center for *jaspe* treadle-loomed weaving. Founded in the sixteenth century, the town is situated on a green undulating plateau and is surrounded by beautiful tree-covered hills. Plains stretch to neighboring towns of Salcajá and San Andrés Xecul. The Samalá River winds along the edge of town and divides the municipality. The festivities of the patron saint, Santiago, are celebrated from July 22 through the 26.

At least since the turn of the century, but probably since colonial times, women of San Cristóbal Totonicapán have worn a ruffled collar called a *gola.* It is decorated with floral emboidery and worn over the top of a plain *huipil* for daily and ceremonial use. O'Neale (1945) reports that the embroidery is done by professionals. The specimen in the Taylor Museum (Figure 141) with its alphabetical and floral designs was executed in a needlepoint stitch. Both design and technique illustrate the unmistakable European origin of the *gola.* Since at least the 1940s, the *gola* has complemented a plain white *huipil* made of commercially loomed cotton for daily

Figure 147. *Cofradía huipil* from Totonicapán, ca. 1930. TM 1013.

wear. Another variation of the daily *huipil*, documented in the collections and literature of the post-1960 period, has replaced the separate *gola*. It is decorated with profuse floral embroidery encircling the neckline in the style of Santa María Chiquimula textiles. A variety of colors is used in the embroidery and ground fabric.

For festive occasions, including *cofradía* rituals and weddings, an elaborately decorated *gola*, which sometimes has two tiers of ruffles covering the shoulders, is customary. A ceremonial *huipil* of the 1930s in the Prentiss N. Gray collection was described by Breuer (1942:14-15) as consisting of three panels of white cotton with white brocaded work of geometric patterns and bird motifs. It also has purple, red, and yellow vertical stripes down the center of the front and back panels. A more contemporary illustration of a San Cristóbal Totonicapán ceremonial *huipil* is provided by Pettersen (1976:31). This piece is nearly identical to the *huipil* from Totonicapán in the Taylor Museum (Figure 146).

Yet another variant of the ceremonial *huipil* described by O'Neale (1945) is made of blue skirt material elaborately embroidered in silk motifs including birds, flowers, dots, and x's. A *gola* and sleeve ruffles are also noted by O'Neale as part of this ceremonial *huipil*.

Because San Cristóbal is a center for the production of treadle-loomed *jaspe* cloth, there is a great deal of variety in the colors and patterns of aprons and shawls and in the lengths of skirts. The wraparound skirts reach to the ankles and are commonly blue and green, although in recent decades bright orange, purple, yellow, turquoise, and magenta have gained popularity. Some of the named *jaspe* patterns used in San Cristóbal Totonicapán include *contra* ("athwart"), *jaspe botado* ("horizontal *ikat*"), *rama* ("branch"), and *cadena* ("chain"). A unique feature in the production of some San Cristóbal *jaspe* is the practice of dyeing dark blue *jaspe* patterns onto colored rather than white yarns. This type of *jaspe* was not found in the collections studied, but is consistently noted in the literature (Anderson 1978:158, O'Neale 1945:264, Osborne 1965:47).

The two tapestry-technique hair ties in the Taylor Museum collection are probably trade items from the municipal capital of Totonicapán.

Santa María Chiquimula

Figure 143. *Huipil* from Totonicapán, ca. 1900. AMNH 65/3879.

TOTONICAPÁN

The women of Santa María Chiquimula are sheep herders. They find a ready market for the raw wool among local weavers and those from the neighboring municipality of Momostenango. The wooded lands of Chiquimula boast an abundance of springs where sheep are watered. Men of the community specialize in the production of pottery, agave fiber cargo nets, and stone masonry. As in most municipalities of the department, the forests are commercially owned and exploited.

A Quiché-speaking community, Santa María Chiquimula has a long history. The Precolumbian ancestors of today's population inhabited the nearby site of Tzoloj Che ("elderberry"). According to ethnohistoric documents, the valiant warriors of Tzoloj Che were subjugated by the Central Quiché of Utatlán in the mid-fifteenth century.

The woman's costume of Santa María Chiquimula is represented in the collections and described in the literature of the 1930s to 1940s, the 1960s and 1970s. Most common is a type of *huipil* which is wide and long with dark blue and red vertical stripes; it sometimes contains white pinstripes. It has a characteristic

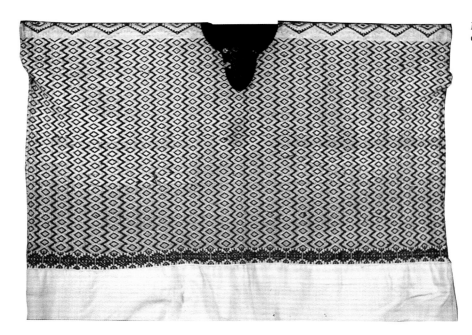

Figure 111. *Huipil* from San Marcos, ca. 1930. TM 650.

Figure 112. *Huipil* from San Marcos, ca. 1975. Alberta 75.2.4.

Figure 113. Skirt fabric from San Pedro Sacatepéquez, ca. 1930. TM 648.

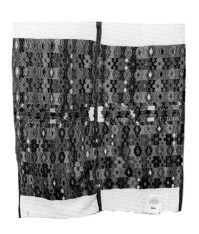

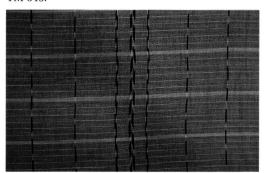

Figure 124. *Huipil* fabric from San Lucas Tolimán, ca. 1930. TM 639.

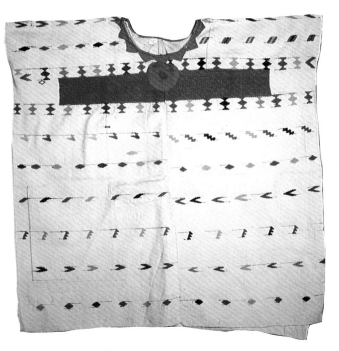

Figure 129. *Huipil* from San Lucas Tolimán, ca. 1900. Lowie 3-151.

Figure 114. Mass *huipil* from Santa Catarina Nahualá, ca. 1930. TM 998.

Figure 139. Ceremonial *huipil* from
Sololá, ca. 1970. Gordon Frost
Collection.

Figure 141. Gola from San Cristóbal
Totonicapán, ca. 1930. TM 1011.

Figure 136. Man's costume from
Santiago Atitlán, ca. 1930. Shirt:
TM 1038, Sash: TM 1037, Hatband
tzute: TM 1039.

Figure 146. Mass *huipil* from Totonicapán, ca. 1930. TM 746.

Figure 134. Detail of *huipil* from Santiago Atitlán, ca. 1970. Gordon Frost Collection.

Figure 137. Blouse and wedding *huipil* from Sololá, ca. 1930. Blouse: TM 638, Wedding *huipil*: TM 635.

gold- and magenta-banded *randa* joining the two panels at the center front and back
(Figure 142). By the 1950s, another style of *huipil* was produced. It is made of white
fabric with a floral embroidered yoke like that described previously from
San Cristóbal Totonicapán. Both *huipil* styles are worn tucked into the skirt and are
bloused to cover the sash. The ankle-length tube skirt is heavy and stiff, and its bulk
is exaggerated by gathering at the waist. A long black woolen braid called a *tocoyal*
encircles the head, its tassels falling behind the ears or in front of the eyes.

TOTONICAPÁN Totonicapán

Totonicapán is the Quiché-speaking capital of the department of the same name.
It has a population of more than 7,000. The municipal terrain is very broken, but
fertile and scenic, with forests of pine, spruce, and oak. The few flat areas at the edge
of town and local mountain slopes are cultivated with wheat, corn, and beans.
Industries of the town include cabinetry, flour milling, pottery making, and the
distilling of brandy.

Totonicapán is a center for treadle-loomed weaving, especially reversal
supplementary weft-decorated fabrics for *huipiles*. These lengths of fabric are mass
produced through the addition of pattern harnesses, which facilitate lifting the warps
for the insertion of the pattern threads. Workshops using the treadle loom have been
prolific producers of *huipil* fabric in a variety of geometric, human, and animal
designs since at least the turn of the century. Today these treadle-loomed *huipil*
fabrics have supplanted those woven on the backstrap loom for daily wear.
Treadle-loomed fabrics, as well as the *huipiles* made from them, are being adopted
throughout the Highlands. For instance, they are worn in Quezaltenango,
San Pedro Sacatepéquez, San Marcos, and San Lucas Tolimán. The type of individual
who wears these trade *huipiles*, that is, his or her social class or status, is a subject
worthy of further investigation.

The collections of the American Museum of Natural History include two
huipiles woven on the backstrap loom and dating to the early 1900s (Figure 143). A
huipil in the Lowie Museum collection dating to the same period (Figure 144)
illustrates the carry over to the treadle loom of design motifs and their arrangement.
Specifically, chevron, zigzag, and dot motifs are organized in bands which reflect
along the horizontal axis so that the design on the front and back is identical. On
both sides of the *huipil* the bands are mirrored on either side of the *pecho*
("breast band"). The backstrap pieces, however, lack the long plain white "tail" of
fabric below the design field. Perhaps this feature developed during the translation of
the style to the treadle loom. Because the time required to produce the longer panels
was reduced, the expense of the additional fabric was offset.

In the collections studied, all of the contemporary (ca. 1960-1970) *huipiles* were
treadle loomed. They differed stylistically from their turn-of-the-century counterparts
in several ways. First, the overall design field was more extensive on the newer
pieces, covering the entire upper half of the *huipil* so that all of the undecorated
ground fabric would be tucked into the skirt. Secondly, contemporary *huipil* fabrics
display different design structures. These have both contiguous horizontal bands and
two-dimensional motif layouts arranged along both horizontal and vertical axes
(Figure 145). This type of patterning has been omitted in the *pecho* band. Finally,

Figure 145. *Huipil* from
Totonicapán, ca. 1970.
UCLA X76-1226, gift of Caroline and
Howard West.

Figure 148. Woman's hair tie and
sashes from Totonicapán, ca. 1930.
Sash (left): TM 755, Hair tie:
TM 1018, Sash: TM 1012.

several of the modern pieces incorporate bands of *jaspe* designs not evident in the
turn-of-the-century pieces.

Two ceremonial *huipil* styles of Totonicapán are represented in the Taylor
Museum collection (Figures 146, 147). Quite different from the daily *huipiles*
described above, they were made to be worn over the top of the skirt and hang
almost to the knees. The ruffled collar and cuffs, embellished with floral embroidery,
are distinctly Spanish in origin. So, too, is the customary white Mass veil worn over
the top of the traditional Totonicapán hair tie. Two pieces labeled by the collector as
a "Mass *huipil*" and a "*cofradía huipil*" (1013, 751) are constructed of white
backstrap-loomed fabric with white supplementary-weft motifs in horizontal bands,
much like that of Quezaltenango ceremonial *huipiles* (Figure 89). This stylistic
sharing is not surprising given the historical ties between the two towns. Both have
been important market centers since Precolumbian times, when they were linked
under the hegemony of the Quiché lords in order to facilitate trade to the capital of
Utatlán.

In addition to treadle-loomed *huipiles*, skirts, shawls, and aprons, Totonicapán
workshops specialize in a type of hair tie that is traded throughout the Highlands
and worn in a variety of ways, depending upon local custom (Figure 148). Woven in
a weft-faced tapestry technique on a narrow, tablelike loom, these hair ties are most
often produced by women and girls. In recent decades rayon has almost entirely
replaced silk for wefts, although patterned cotton pieces continue to be made for
everyday wear. Patterning on all hair ties is quite standardized, as would be expected
of such mass-produced trade items. Bands of diamonds, zigzags, chevrons, and
stripes are combined with figures of humans, birds, and rabbits in repeating
sequences of from two to five colors per piece. Hair ties for ceremonial or festive
occasions are generally longer and more elaborately patterned, with either real or
imitation silver threads wound around the loops that hold the pompons at each end.

A special, very narrow backstrap loom is used for making the stiff sash worn by
women (Figure 148). Bands of multiunit geometric motifs are created by floating
pairs of warps over the weft threads.

· Figure 144. *Huipil* from
Totonicapán, ca. 1900. Lowie 3-65.

Figure 142. Woman's costume from
Santa María Chiquimula, ca. 1930.
Huipil: TM 659, *Tzute*: TM 655,
Hair tie: TM 837.

APPENDIX
Catalogue of the Taylor Museum's
E. B. Ricketson Collection of Guatemalan Textiles

■ **Rabinal, Baja Verapaz**
MASS *HUIPIL* ca. 1930
TM 716 (*Taylor Museum identification number*)
Loom: backstrap
Pattern and Materials: <u>ground fabric</u>: 2/3 (2 warp/3 weft),
2/1, and 2/2 plain weaves—cotton
<u>brocade</u>: reversal—cotton, silk
Colors: <u>ground fabric</u>: white
<u>brocade</u>: red, yellow, green, blue green, dark purple

■ **San Miguel Chicaj, Baja Verapaz**
MAN'S JACKET ca. 1930 (*Illustrated Figure 13*)
TM 712
Loom: treadle
Pattern and Materials: <u>ground fabric</u>: striped 1/1 and 2/2
plain weaves and plain twill weave—cotton, wool
<u>embroidery</u>: stem and chain stitches—silk
Colors: <u>ground fabric</u>: red, dark brown, white
<u>embroidery</u>: yellow, blue green, light blue, dark blue,
violet, magenta, white

MASS *HUIPIL* ca. 1930 (*Illustrated Figure 8*)
TM 718
Loom: backstrap
Pattern and Materials: <u>ground fabric</u>: 1/1, 2/2, and 1/2 plain
weaves, horizontal ribbing—cotton
<u>brocade</u>: reversal—cotton
Colors: <u>ground fabric</u>: white
<u>brocade</u>: red, yellow, violet, white

■ **San Gabriel Pansuj, Baja Verapaz**
HUIPIL ca. 1930
TM 717
Loom: backstrap
Pattern and Materials: <u>ground fabric</u>: 1/1 plain weave,
horizontal ribbing—cotton
<u>brocade</u>: single-faced and reversal—cotton
Colors: <u>ground fabric</u>: white
<u>brocade</u>: red, yellow, green, blue

■ **Acatenango, Chimaltenango**
HUIPIL ca. 1930 (*Illustrated Figure 14*)
TM 715
Loom: backstrap
Pattern and Materials: <u>ground fabric</u>: striped 4/4 plain
weave—cotton
<u>brocade</u>: picked reversal—cotton, silk
Colors: <u>ground fabric</u>: red, white
<u>brocade</u>: red, orange, yellow, blue, purple, magenta

■ **San Antonio Nejapa, Chimaltenango**
HUIPIL ca. 1930
TM 605
Loom: backstrap
Pattern and Materials: <u>ground fabric</u>: 2/1, 2/2 and 1/1 plain
weaves, horizontal ribbing—cotton
<u>brocade</u>: reversal—cotton, silk
Colors: <u>ground fabric</u>: white
<u>brocade</u>: red, yellow, violet

■ **San Juan Comalapa, Chimaltenango**
HUIPIL ca. 1930 (*Illustrated Figure 15*)
TM 773
Loom: backstrap
Pattern and Materials: <u>ground fabric</u>: checked 1/1 and
weft-faced plain weaves—cotton
<u>brocade</u>: reversal—silk, wool
Colors: <u>ground fabric</u>: red, pink, brown, yellow, dark green,
blue, purple, violet, white, black
<u>brocade</u>: orange, yellow, light yellow, magenta, purple,
blue green, blue, white

WOMAN'S SASH ca. 1930 (*Illustrated Figure 15*)
TM 761
Loom: backstrap
Pattern and Materials: <u>ground fabric</u>: striped warp-faced
plain weave—cotton, wool
Colors: <u>ground fabric</u>: red, pink, green, blue, purple, white

SKIRT ca. 1930 (*Illustrated Figure 15*)
TM 770
Loom: treadle
Pattern and Materials: <u>ground fabric</u>: plaid 3/2 and 2/2
plain weaves—cotton
Colors: <u>ground fabric</u>: blue, white

CEREMONIAL *SERVILLETA* ca. 1930
TM 766
Loom: backstrap
Pattern and Materials: <u>ground fabric</u>: plaid 1/1 plain
weave—cotton

brocade: reversal—silk, wool
Colors: ground fabric: red, yellow, dark green, blue, white
brocade: pink, orange, yellow, blue green, light blue, purple, magenta, white

■ **San José Poaquil, Chimaltenango**
HUIPIL ca. 1930 (Illustrated Figure 19)
TM 767
Loom: backstrap
Pattern and Materials: ground fabric: 1/1 and 1/3 plain weaves—cotton
brocade: reversal—silk, wool
embroidery: buttonhole stitch—silk
Colors: ground fabric: red, light pink, brown, yellow, blue, light blue, magenta, white
brocade: pink, light pink, yellow, green, dark green, blue green, blue, light blue, magenta, black
embroidery: purple

■ **San Martín Jilotepeque, Chimaltenango**
HUIPIL ca. 1930
TM 614
Loom: backstrap
Pattern and Materials: ground fabric: 2/2 plain weave—cotton
brocade: reversal—silk
Colors: ground fabric: dark blue
brocade: yellow, blue green, blue, purple, magenta, white

INSIDE HUIPIL ca. 1930
TM 826
Loom: backstrap
Pattern and Materials: ground fabric: 1/1 and 1/2 plain weaves—cotton
brocade: single-faced—cotton, silk
embroidery: buttonhole stitch—cotton
Colors: ground fabric: red, white
brocade: red, yellow, green, dark blue, purple
embroidery: green

HUIPIL ca. 1930 (Illustrated Figure 21)
TM 613
Loom: backstrap
Pattern and Materials: ground fabric: 2/2 plain weave—cotton
brocade: reversal—cotton, silk
embroidery: stem stitch—cotton, silk
trim: taffeta ribbon
Colors: ground fabric: dark blue
brocade: red, yellow, blue green, blue, purple, lavender, magenta, white
embroidery: yellow, purple, white
trim: pink

TZUTE ca. 1930
TM 615
Loom: backstrap
Pattern and Materials: ground fabric: 2/2 plain weave—cotton
brocade: single-faced and reversal—silk, lustrina
trim: tassels—cotton
Colors: ground fabric: dark blue
brocade: yellow, blue green, blue gray, violet, magenta, white
trim: pink

TZUTE ca. 1930
TM 1007
Loom: backstrap
Pattern and Materials: ground fabric: ikat-striped warp-faced plain weave—cotton, silk
brocade: single-faced—silk
Colors: ground fabric: red, blue green, light blue, dark blue, purple
brocade: yellow, blue green, purple, white

■ **Santa Apolonia, Chimaltenango**
WORK HUIPIL ca. 1930
TM 606
Loom: backstrap
Pattern and Materials: ground fabric: 2/2 plain weave—cotton
embroidery: stem and buttonhole stitches—cotton
Colors: ground fabric: white
embroidery: red, yellow, green

COFRADÍA HUIPIL ca. 1900-1920 (Illustrated Figure 25)
TM 607
Loom: backstrap
Pattern and Materials: ground fabric: 1/1 and 1/2 plain weaves—cotton
brocade: reversal—cotton, silk
trim: ribbon—silk
Colors: ground fabric: white
brocade: light pink, yellow, light green, violet
trim: pink

WOMAN'S HEADBAND IMPORTED FROM TOTONICAPÁN ca. 1930
TM 833
Loom: small treadle loom
Pattern and Materials: ground fabric: weft-faced plain weave—cotton
trim: pompons and tassels—silk
Colors: ground fabric: red, yellow, dark green, dark blue, purple, white, black
trim: red, yellow, blue green, blue, purple, black

WOMAN'S TZUTE ca. 1930

TM 801
Pattern and Materials: <u>ground fabric</u>: 1/1 plain weave, commercially milled—cotton
Colors: <u>ground fabric</u>: white

■ **Tecpán, Chimaltenango**
WORK *HUIPIL* ca. 1930 (*Illustrated Figure 27*)
TM 764
Loom: backstrap
Pattern and Materials: <u>ground fabric</u>: striped warp-faced plain weave—cotton
<u>brocade</u>: single-faced—cotton
Colors: <u>ground fabric</u>: red, yellow, dark green, dark blue, white
<u>brocade</u>: dark blue

HUIPIL ca. 1930
TM 771
Loom: backstrap
Pattern and Materials: <u>ground fabric</u>: striped warp-faced and 2/2 plain weaves—cotton
<u>brocade</u>: single-faced and reversal—cotton, silk
Colors: <u>ground fabric</u>: red, brown, yellow
<u>brocade</u>: orange, yellow, blue green, light blue, dark blue, purple, violet, magenta, white

HUIPIL ca. 1930 (*Illustrated Figure 27*)
TM 772
Loom: backstrap
Pattern and Materials: <u>ground fabric</u>: striped warp-faced plain weave—cotton
<u>brocade</u>: single-faced—cotton, silk
<u>trim</u>: taffeta ribbon
Colors: <u>ground fabric</u>: red, brown, yellow, dark green
<u>brocade</u>: pink, yellow, blue green, light blue, purple, magenta, white
<u>trim</u>: pink

WOMAN'S SASH ca. 1930 (*Illustrated Figure 27*)
TM 762
Loom: backstrap
Pattern and Materials: <u>ground fabric</u>: warp-faced plain weave—cotton
<u>brocade</u>: single-faced and reversal—silk
Colors: <u>ground fabric</u>: red, yellow, dark green
<u>brocade</u>: yellow, blue green, blue, purple, magenta, white

SERVILLETA ca. 1930
TM 768
Loom: backstrap
Pattern and Materials: <u>ground fabric</u>: striped warp-faced plain weave—cotton
Colors: <u>ground fabric</u>: red, yellow, dark blue, white

SERVILLETA ca. 1930

TM 765
Loom: backstrap
Pattern and Materials: <u>ground fabric</u>: checked 2/2 plain weave—cotton
Colors: <u>ground fabric</u>: red, yellow, dark blue, white

■ **San Andrés Itzapa, Chimaltenango**
HUIPIL ca. 1930 (*Illustrated Figure 30*)
TM 610
Loom: backstrap
Pattern and Materials: <u>ground fabric</u>: 3/3 plain weave—cotton
<u>brocade</u>: single-faced—cotton, silk
Colors: <u>ground fabric</u>: dark blue
<u>brocade</u>: orange, yellow, dark green, purple, magenta, white

HUIPIL FABRIC ca. 1930 (*Illustrated Figure 30*)
TM 608
Loom: backstrap
Pattern and Materials: <u>ground fabric</u>: 3/3 plain weave—cotton
<u>brocade</u>: single-faced—silk
Colors: <u>ground fabric</u>: dark green
<u>brocade</u>: dark brown, yellow, blue green, purple, magenta, white

■ **Santa Cruz Balanyá, Chimaltenango**
HUIPIL ca. 1930 (*Illustrated Figure 32*)
TM 720
Loom: backstrap
Pattern and Materials: <u>ground fabric</u>: 2/2 plain weave and weft looping (*chivo*, cf. p. 49)—cotton
<u>embroidery</u>: stem, randa and satin stitches—silk, wool
Colors: <u>ground fabric</u>: dark blue, white
<u>embroidery</u>: pink, dark green, blue

■ **Palín, Escuintla**
HUIPIL ca. 1930
TM 612
Loom: backstrap
Pattern and Materials: <u>ground fabric</u>: 1/1 and warp-faced plain weaves—cotton
<u>brocade</u>: reversal—cotton, silk
<u>embroidery</u>: running stitch—cotton, silk
Colors: <u>ground fabric</u>: red, white
<u>brocade</u>: red, yellow, pale yellow, dark green, turquoise, blue, magenta
<u>embroidery</u>: red, yellow, pale yellow, dark green, turquoise, blue, magenta, black

HUIPIL ca. 1930 (*Illustrated Figure 33*)
TM 611
Loom: backstrap
Pattern and Materials: <u>ground fabric</u>: 1/1 and warp-faced

plain weaves—cotton
brocade: reversal—cotton
embroidery: fake satin, stem, running stitches—cotton
Colors: ground fabric: red, white
brocade: red, blue
embroidery: red, yellow, green, dark green, blue, violet

WOMAN'S SASH ca. 1930 (*Illustrated Figure 33*)
TM 831
Loom: backstrap
Pattern and Materials: ground fabric: striped warp-faced
plain weave—cotton
brocade: single-faced—silk, wool
Colors: ground fabric: red, dark blue
brocade: pink, yellow, turquoise, purple, magenta, beige

■ **Mixco, Guatemala**
COFRADÍA HUIPIL ca. 1910 (*Illustrated Figure 38*)
TM 753
Loom: backstrap
Pattern and Materials: ground fabric: 1/1 and 1/3 plain
weaves—cotton
embroidery: satin, stem, cross, closed herringbone and
interlocking running stitches—cotton
trim: metal sequins, cotton lace and silk ribbon
Colors: ground fabric: white
embroidery: violet
trim: gold (sequins), violet and white (lace), purple
(ribbon)

HUIPIL FABRIC ca. 1930 (*Illustrated Figure 36*)
TM 1028
Loom: backstrap
Pattern and Materials: ground fabric: 3/3 plain weave—
cotton
brocade: single-faced—cotton
Colors: ground fabric: red, white
brocade: red, yellow, olive, dark blue, violet

SKIRT ca. 1930 (*Illustrated Figure 36*)
TM 1031
Loom: treadle
Pattern and Materials: ground fabric: plaid weft and warp
ikat, 1/1 plain weave—cotton
trim: seam binding—wool
Colors: ground fabric: dark blue, white
trim: black

WOMAN'S *TZUTE* ca. 1930
TM 1030
Loom: backstrap
Pattern and Materials: ground fabric: striped 1/2 plain
weave and plain twill weave—cotton
border: knotted fringe with tassels—cotton

Colors: ground fabric: dark blue, white
border: dark blue, white

WOMAN'S SASH ca. 1930 (*Illustrated Figure 36*)
TM 1027
Loom: backstrap
Pattern and Materials: ground fabric: 2/1 warp-faced plain
weave and 1/1 plain weave with warp floats—cotton,
wool
Colors: ground fabric: red, pale green, white

SHAWL ca. 1930
TM 680
Loom: treadle
Pattern and Materials: ground fabric: plain twill weave,
commercially milled—cotton
Colors: ground fabric: white

FIESTA SHAWL ca. 1930
TM 1029
Loom: treadle
Pattern and Materials: ground fabric: 1/1 plain weave—
cotton
Colors: ground fabric: white

■ **San Juan Sacatepéquez, Guatemala**
HUIPIL ca. 1930 (*Illustrated Figure 40*)
TM 1034
Loom: backstrap
Pattern and Materials: ground fabric: striped warp-faced
plain weave—cotton
brocade: reversal—cotton, silk
Colors: ground fabric: red, brown, yellow, green, blue,
violet, white
brocade: red, yellow, turquoise, purple, violet, magenta
embroidery: magenta

COFRADÍA HUIPIL ca. 1930 (*Illustrated Figure 43*)
TM 823
Loom: backstrap
Pattern and Materials: ground fabric: 2/2 plain weave,
horizontal ribbing—cotton
brocade: reversal—cotton
embroidery: randa stitch—cotton, silk
appliqué and trim: taffeta ribbon
Colors: ground fabric: white
brocade: red, violet
embroidery: violet, magenta
trim: blue

SKIRT ca. 1930 (*Illustrated Figure 40*)
TM 1035
Loom: treadle
Pattern and Materials: ground fabric: checked 2/2 plain
weave—cotton

embroidery: randa stitch—cotton and silk or rayon
Colors: ground fabric: dark blue, white
embroidery: violet, magenta

WOMAN'S SASH ca. 1930 (*Illustrated Figure 40*)
TM 1033
Loom: backstrap
Pattern and Materials: ground fabric: striped warp-faced
plain weave—cotton
brocade: reversal—cotton, silk
Colors: ground fabric: red, yellow, violet
brocade: yellow, green, purple, violet, white, black

SASH ca. 1930
TM 828
Loom: backstrap
Pattern and Materials: ground fabric: striped warp-faced
plain weave—cotton
brocade: reversal—silk
Colors: ground fabric: red, yellow, violet
brocade: yellow, magenta

WOMAN'S *TZUTE* ca. 1930
TM 1032
Loom: backstrap
Pattern and Materials: ground fabric: 3/3 and warp-faced
plain weaves—cotton
brocade: reversal—cotton, silk
Colors: ground fabric: dark blue, violet
brocade: orange, yellow, purple, violet, magenta, white

MAN'S COAT ca. 1930
TM 829
Loom: treadle
Pattern and Materials: ground fabric: warp-faced plain
weave—cotton
trim: commercial braiding, felted plain twill weave
(collar)—wool
lining: plain twill weave, commercially milled—cotton
Colors: ground fabric: red, brown, yellow, violet
trim: black
lining: white

MAN'S *COFRADÍA* SHIRT ca. 1930
TM 830
Loom: backstrap
Pattern and Materials: ground fabric: striped warp-faced
plain weave—cotton
Colors: ground fabric: red, brown, yellow, violet, white

MAN'S *COFRADÍA TZUTE* ca. 1930 (*Illustrated Figure 50*)
TM 822
Loom: backstrap
Pattern and Materials: ground fabric: striped warp-faced
plain weave—cotton

brocade: reversal—cotton and silk or rayon
embroidery: randa stitch—cotton and silk or rayon
Colors: ground fabric: red, yellow, violet
brocade: yellow, green, blue, violet, white, black
embroidery: red, yellow, green, blue, purple, violet,
white

MAN'S *COFRADÍA SERVILLETA* ca. 1930
TM 825
Loom: backstrap
Pattern and Materials: ground fabric: striped 3/3 and 1/3
plain weaves—cotton
brocade: reversal—cotton, silk
Colors: ground fabric: red, yellow, violet
brocade: orange, yellow, dark green, blue green, blue,
dark blue, purple, violet, magenta, white

■ **San Pedro Sacatepéquez, Guatemala**
HUIPIL FABRIC ca. 1930 (*Illustrated Figure 48*)
TM 824
Loom: backstrap
Pattern and Materials: ground fabric: 3/3 plain weave—
cotton
brocade: single-faced—cotton, silk
Colors: ground fabric: red, violet, white
brocade: red, yellow, green, purple, violet, magenta

HUIPIL ca. 1930
TM 743
Loom: backstrap
Pattern and Materials: ground fabric: striped 3/3 plain
weave—cotton
brocade: reversal—cotton, silk
Colors: ground fabric: red, blue, white
brocade: red, yellow, dark green, purple, magenta

FIESTA *HUIPIL* ca. 1930 (*Illustrated Figure 44*)
TM 737
Loom: backstrap
Pattern and Materials: ground fabric: 3/3 plain weave—
cotton
brocade: reversal—cotton
Colors: ground fabric: red, violet, white
brocade: red, violet

SKIRT ca. 1930 (*Illustrated Figure 44*)
TM 745
Loom: treadle
Pattern and Materials: ground fabric: plaid 2,3/2,3 plain
weave—cotton
embroidery: randa stitch—cotton
Colors: ground fabric: dark blue, white
embroidery: red, violet

WOMAN'S SASH ca. 1930 (*Illustrated Figure 44*)
TM 741

Loom: backstrap
Pattern and Materials: <u>ground fabric</u>: 3/3 plain weave—
cotton
<u>brocade</u>: reversal—cotton
Colors: <u>ground fabric</u>: dark blue
<u>brocade</u>: red, yellow, turquoise, purple, violet,
magenta, white

■ **San Pedro Chuarrancho, Guatemala**
HUIPIL ca. 1930 (*Illustrated Figure 46*)
TM 744
Loom: backstrap
Pattern and Materials: <u>ground fabric</u>: 3/3 and 1/2 plain
weave—cotton
<u>brocade</u>: reversal—cotton, silk
<u>embroidery</u>: overcast and randa stitches—cotton, silk
Colors: <u>ground fabric</u>: white
<u>brocade</u>: red, light blue, purple, violet
<u>embroidery</u>: violet

SASH ca. 1930
TM 738
Loom: backstrap
Pattern and Materials: <u>ground fabric</u>: warp-faced plain
weave—wool
<u>brocade</u>: reversal—wool
Colors: <u>ground fabric</u>: white
<u>brocade</u>: red, pink, blue green, violet

■ **San Pedro Ayampuc, Guatemala**
HUIPIL FABRIC ca. 1930 (*Illustrated Figure 53*)
TM 763
Loom: backstrap
Pattern and Materials: <u>ground fabric</u>: 3/3,4 plain weave—
cotton
<u>brocade</u>: reversal—cotton, silk
Colors: <u>ground fabric</u>: white
<u>brocade</u>: red, yellow, turquoise, dark blue, purple,
magenta

COFRADÍA HUIPIL ca. 1930 (*Illustrated Figure 47*)
TM 769
Loom: backstrap
Pattern and Materials: <u>ground fabric</u>: 3/3 plain weave—
cotton
<u>brocade</u>: reversal—cotton, silk
<u>embroidery</u>: randa stitch—cotton
Colors: <u>ground fabric</u>: white
<u>brocade</u>: red, yellow, green, purple, magenta
<u>embroidery</u>: red

HUIPIL ca. 1930 (*Illustrated Figure 52*)
TM 758
Loom: backstrap
Pattern and Materials: <u>ground fabric</u>: 2/4 plain weave—
cotton

<u>brocade</u>: single-faced and reversal—cotton, silk
<u>embroidery</u>: running and satin stitches—cotton, silk
<u>trim</u>: velvet—cotton
Colors: <u>ground fabric</u>: red, blue
<u>brocade</u>: pink, peach, yellow, pale yellow, green
turquoise, blue, blue gray, purple, magenta, white
<u>embroidery</u>: pink, pale yellow, green, turquoise,
purple, magenta
<u>trim</u>: black

COFRADÍA TZUTE ca. 1930
TM 759
Loom: backstrap
Pattern and Materials: <u>ground fabric</u>: 2/2 plain weave—
cotton
<u>brocade</u>: reversal—cotton, silk
<u>embroidery</u>: stem and satin stitches—cotton, silk
Colors: <u>ground fabric</u>: red
<u>brocade</u>: yellow, green, blue, white
<u>embroidery</u>: yellow, green, blue, purple, magenta,
white

SERVILLETA ca. 1930
TM 760
Loom: backstrap
Pattern and Materials: <u>ground fabric</u>: 3/3 plain weave—
cotton
<u>brocade</u>: single-faced and reversal—cotton, silk
Colors: <u>ground fabric</u>: white
<u>brocade</u>: red, peach, yellow, green, blue, purple, violet,
magenta, black

■ **Santo Tomás Chichicastenango, El Quiché**
HUIPIL ca. 1930 (*Illustrated Figure 54*)
TM 623
Loom: backstrap
Pattern and Materials: <u>ground fabric</u>: striped 1/1 and 1/2
plain weaves—cotton
<u>brocade</u>: picked reversal—silk, wool
<u>embroidery</u>: buttonhole join and chain stitches—silk,
cotton
<u>trim</u>: taffeta ribbon
Colors: <u>ground fabric</u>: brown, white
<u>brocade</u>: dark red, orange, yellow, blue green, purple,
white
<u>embroidery</u>: orange, purple
<u>trim</u>: black

CHRISTENING *HUIPIL* ca. 1930 (*Illustrated Figure 54*)
TM 624
Loom: backstrap
Pattern and Materials: <u>ground fabric</u>: warp-faced plain
weave—cotton

brocade: picked reversal—silk
embroidery: buttonhole join and chain stitches—silk
Colors: ground fabric: white
brocade: orange, blue, green, purple
embroidery: orange, dark blue, purple

WOMAN'S SASH ca. 1930 (*Illustrated Figure 54*)
TM 626
Loom: backstrap
Pattern and Materials: ground fabric: striped warp-faced
plain weave—wool
embroidery: satin and chain stitches—silk
trim: tassels—cotton, silk
Colors: ground fabric: white, black
embroidery: orange, light yellow, blue green, purple,
magenta, white
trim: red, orange, blue green, purple

WOMAN'S WEDDING HEADBAND ca. 1930
TM 834
Loom: backstrap
Pattern and Materials: ground fabric: weft-faced plain
weave—wool, silk
trim: tassels—silk
Colors: ground fabric: red, orange, dark brown, violet
trim: violet

TZUTE FOR CARRYING BABY ca. 1930
TM 617
Loom: backstrap
Pattern and Materials: ground fabric: striped 2/2 and warp-
faced plain weaves—cotton
embroidery: buttonhole join and stem stitches—silk
Colors: ground fabric: red, dark blue, white
embroidery: orange, blue green, purple

MAN'S JACKET ca. 1930 (*Illustrated Figure 56*)
TM 1008
Loom: treadle
Pattern and Materials: ground fabric: felted plain twill
weave—wool
embroidery: satin and chain stitches—silk
trim: taffeta ribbon, tassels—silk
Colors: ground fabric: dark brown
embroidery: orange, yellow, light yellow, blue green,
blue, magenta
trim: black (ribbon), orange, blue green, purple,
magenta (tassels)

MAN'S SASH ca. 1930 (*Illustrated Figure 56*)
TM 1010
Loom: backstrap
Pattern and Materials: ground fabric: warp-faced plain
weave—cotton
brocade: reversal—silk

embroidery: stem stitch—silk
Colors: ground fabric: red
brocade: purple
embroidery: orange, yellow, green, blue, white

MAN'S TROUSERS ca. 1930 (*Illustrated Figure 56*)
TM 1009
Loom: treadle
Pattern and Materials: ground fabric: felted 1/1 plain
weave—wool
embroidery: satin and chain stitches—silk
Colors: ground fabric: dark brown
embroidery: orange, yellow, blue, purple

MAN'S BLANKET ca. 1930 (*Illustrated Figure 56*)
TM 616
Loom: treadle
Pattern and Materials: ground fabric: weft-faced plain
weave and plain twill weave—wool
Colors: ground fabric: red, dark brown, dark blue, white

MAN'S TZUTE ca. 1930 (*Illustrated Figure 56*)
TM 1006
Loom: backstrap
Pattern and Materials: ground fabric: 1/1 plain weave—
cotton
brocade: reversal—silk
trim: tassels—silk
Colors: ground fabric: white
brocade: violet
trim: orange, violet

■ Chiché, El Quiché
HUIPIL FABRIC ca. 1930
TM 622
Loom: backstrap
Pattern and Materials: ground fabric: 1/1 plain weave,
horizontal and vertical ribbing—cotton
Colors: ground fabric: white

HUIPIL FABRIC ca. 1930
TM 621
Loom: backstrap
Pattern and Materials: ground fabric: 1/1 plain weave,
horizontal and vertical ribbing—cotton
Colors: ground fabric: white

HUIPIL FABRIC ca. 1930
TM 618
Loom: backstrap
Pattern and Materials: ground fabric: 1/1 plain weave—
cotton
Colors: ground fabric: white

MAN'S SHIRT ca. 1930 (*Illustrated Figure 57*)
TM 620

Pattern and Materials: <u>ground fabric</u>: 1/1 plain weave, commercially milled—cotton
Colors: <u>ground fabric</u>: white

MAN'S SHIRT ca. 1930
TM 1025
Pattern and Materials: <u>ground fabric</u>: striped 1/1 plain weave, commercially milled—cotton
Colors: <u>ground fabric</u>: red, pink, yellow, blue, white

TROUSERS ca. 1930 (*Illustrated Figure 57*)
TM 1024
Pattern and Materials: <u>ground fabric</u>: 1/1 plain weave, commercially milled—cotton
Colors: <u>ground fabric</u>: white

MAN'S JACKET ca. 1930 (*Illustrated Figure 57*)
TM 1026
Loom: treadle
Pattern and Materials: <u>ground fabric</u>: felted, plain twill weave—wool
<u>lining</u>: 1/1 plain weave, commercially milled—cotton
Colors: <u>ground fabric</u>: blue, dark blue, beige
<u>lining</u>: white

MAN'S APRON ca. 1930 (*Illustrated Figure 57*)
TM 1023
Loom: treadle
Pattern and Materials: <u>ground fabric</u>: checked 1/1 felted plain weave—wool
Colors: <u>ground fabric</u>: dark blue, white

■ **Zacualpa, El Quiché**
SHAWL ca. 1930
TM 776
Loom: backstrap
Pattern and Materials: <u>ground fabric</u>: striped warp-faced plain weave—cotton
<u>embroidery</u>: running and randa stitches—silk
Colors: <u>ground fabric</u>: red, orange, yellow, dark green
<u>embroidery</u>: yellow, blue green, purple, magenta, white

■ **Santa Cruz del Quiché, El Quiché**
MAN'S SASH ca. 1930
TM 625
Pattern and Materials: <u>ground fabric</u>: warp-faced plain weave—cotton
Colors: <u>ground fabric</u>: red, white, black

■ **Sacapulas, El Quiché**
WORK *HUIPIL* ca. 1930
TM 780
Pattern and Materials: <u>ground fabric</u>: 1/1 plain weave, commercially milled—cotton
<u>trim</u>: cotton cloth
Colors: <u>ground fabric</u>: white

<u>embroidery</u>: black (machine-stitched)
<u>trim</u>: black

FIESTA *HUIPIL* ca. 1930 (*Illustrated Figure 62*)
TM 791
Loom: backstrap
Pattern and Materials: <u>ground fabric</u>: weft-faced plain weave—cotton
<u>brocade</u>: double-faced—cotton
<u>embroidery</u>: buttonhole join, backstitch, stem, satin and chain stitches—silk
<u>trim</u>: silk cloth
Colors: <u>ground fabric</u>: white
<u>brocade</u>: red, tan, yellow, dark green
<u>embroidery</u>: pink, orange, light blue green
<u>trim</u>: pink

WOMEN'S HEADBANDS ca. 1930 (*TM 785 Illustrated Figure 62*)
TM 784, 785, 978
Loom: backstrap
Pattern and Materials: <u>ground fabric</u>: striped warp-faced (784, 978) and weft-faced (785) plain weaves—cotton (978, 785) and silk (784)
<u>brocade</u>: double-faced—cotton (785)
<u>tassels</u>: cotton (785, 978), silk (784, 978)
Colors: <u>ground fabric</u>: magenta, white (784), red, yellow (785), red, white (978)
<u>brocade</u>: yellow, dark green (785)
<u>tassels</u>: orange, blue green, purple, magenta (784), red, yellow, dark green (785), red, orange, dark green, blue green, purple, magenta (978)

FIESTA TABLECLOTH ca. 1930
TM 790
Loom: backstrap
Pattern and Materials: <u>ground fabric</u>: striped 1/4 and weft-faced plain weaves, horizontal ribbing—cotton, silk
<u>brocade</u>: reversal—silk
<u>embroidery</u>: buttonhole join—cotton, silk
Colors: <u>ground fabric</u>: white
<u>brocade</u>: red, gold, light yellow, green, light blue green
<u>embroidery</u>: red, yellow, magenta

■ **Joyabaj, El Quiché**
HUIPIL ca. 1930 (*Illustrated Figure 60*)
TM 619
Loom: backstrap
Pattern and Materials: <u>ground fabric</u>: striped warp-faced and 2/2 plain weaves—cotton
<u>embroidery</u>: satin, chain, buttonhole, and feather stitches—silk
Colors: <u>ground fabric</u>: red, brown, green, dark blue, white
<u>embroidery</u>: yellow, green, purple, white

■ **San Juan Cotzal, El Quiché**

HUIPIL ca. 1930
TM 793
Loom: backstrap
Pattern and Materials: ground fabric: striped warp-faced and weft-faced plain weaves—cotton
brocade: single-faced (float and weft-wrap)—cotton, silk
embroidery: chain stitch—cotton, wool
trim: cotton cloth
Colors: ground fabric: red, white
brocade: red, orange, yellow, dark green, blue green, purple, white
embroidery: red, yellow, dark green, purple
trim: red

HUIPIL ca. 1930 (*Illustrated Figure 63*)
TM 792
Loom: backstrap
Pattern and Materials: ground fabric: striped warp-faced and weft-faced plain weaves—cotton
brocade: single-faced (float and weft-wrap)—cotton, wool, silk
embroidery: chain stitch—cotton, wool
trim: cotton cloth
Colors: ground fabric: red, orange, yellow, dark green, white
brocade: red, pink, orange, yellow, dark green, light blue, purple, violet, magenta, white
embroidery: orange, yellow, dark green, violet
trim: red

WOMAN'S SASH ca. 1930 (*Illustrated Figure 63*)
TM 779
Loom: backstrap
Pattern and Materials: ground fabric: striped warp-faced plain weave—cotton
Colors: ground fabric: red, green white

WOMAN'S *SERVILLETA* ca. 1930 (*Illustrated Figure 63*)
TM 781
Loom: backstrap
Pattern and Materials: ground fabric: striped warp-faced plain weave—cotton
brocade: single-faced (float and weft-wrap) weave—cotton, silk
Colors: ground fabric: red, orange, yellow, dark green, white
brocade: orange, yellow, light yellow, light blue green, purple, violet

WOMAN'S SHAWL ca. 1930
TM 787
Loom: backstrap
Pattern and Materials: ground fabric: striped warp-faced

plain weave—cotton
brocade: single-faced (float and weft-wrap)—cotton, silk, wool
Colors: ground fabric: red, yellow, green, dark blue
brocade: pink, orange, yellow, green, light blue green, purple, violet, white

MAN'S JACKET ca. 1930
TM 775
Loom: treadle
Pattern and Materials: ground fabric: striped warp-faced plain weave—cotton
lining: 1/1, commercially milled—cotton
trim: braiding—wool
Colors: ground fabric: red, black
lining: white
trim: black

MAN'S SASH ca. 1930
TM 782
Loom: backstrap
Pattern and Materials: ground fabric: striped warp-faced plain weave—cotton
brocade: single-faced (float and weft-wrap)—silk
Colors: ground fabric: red
brocade: pink, orange, yellow, light blue green, purple, violet

MAN'S SASH ca. 1930
TM 778
Loom: backstrap
Pattern and Materials: ground fabric: striped warp-faced plain weave—cotton
brocade: single-faced (float and weft-wrap)—silk
Colors: ground fabric: red
brocade: orange, light blue green, purple, violet, white

MAN'S SASH ca. 1930
TM 777
Loom: backstrap
Pattern and Materials: ground fabric: striped warp-faced plain weave—cotton
brocade: single-faced (float and weft-wrap)—silk
Colors: ground fabric: red
brocade: light yellow, light green, purple, lavender, white

■ **Aguacatán, Huehuetenango**

HUIPIL ca. 1930
TM 676
Pattern and Materials: ground fabric: plain weave, commercially milled—cotton
embroidery: chain and satin stitches—silk
trim: cotton cloth

Colors: ground fabric: white
embroidery: yellow, light blue, purple, magenta
trim: red

SKIRT ca. 1930
TM 786
Loom: treadle or backstrap
Pattern and Materials: ground fabric: striped warp-faced
plain weave—cotton
Colors: ground fabric: red, yellow, dark blue

WOMAN'S SASH ca. 1930
TM 684
Loom: backstrap
Pattern and Materials: ground fabric: warp-faced plain
weave—cotton
Colors: ground fabric: dark brown, beige

WOMAN'S HEADBAND IMPORTED FROM COTZAL
ca. 1930
TM 783
Loom: backstrap
Pattern and Materials: ground fabric: warp-faced plain
weave—cotton
brocade: single-faced—silk
Colors: ground fabric: red
brocade: yellow, light blue green, purple

■ **Chiantla, Huehuetenango**
SKIRT ca. 1930
TM 653
Loom: treadle
Pattern and Materials: ground fabric: solid- and *ikat*-striped
1/1 plain weave—cotton
Colors: ground fabric: red, yellow, green, dark blue, white

■ **Jacaltenango, Huehuetenango**
HUIPIL ca. 1930 (*Illustrated Figure 66*)
TM 803
Loom: backstrap
Pattern and Materials: ground fabric: 2/2 plain weave,
horizontal ribbing—cotton
brocade: single-faced—cotton
trim: eyelet, ribbon and rickrack, commercially
milled—cotton
Colors: ground fabric: white
brocade: dark blue
trims: white (eyelet), orange (rickrack), pink, peach,
blue, purple (taffeta ribbon), blue, white (embroidered
ribbon)

WOMEN'S HEADBANDS ca. 1930
TM 798, 799, 800
Loom: backstrap
Pattern and Materials: ground fabric: striped 2/2 plain
weave—cotton

brocade: double-faced—cotton, wool, silk (798) cotton,
wool (799, 800)
Colors: ground fabric: red, yellow, dark green (798, 799,
800)
brocade: pink, green, blue, purple, magenta, white
(798), red, pink, orange, yellow, green, blue, purple
(799), orange, yellow, green, light green, blue, dark
blue, purple, magenta, white (800)

GIRL'S HEADBAND ca. 1930
TM 797
Loom: backstrap
Pattern and Materials: ground fabric: striped 2/2 plain
weave—cotton
brocade: double-faced—cotton
trim: tassels—cotton
Colors: ground fabric: red, orange, yellow, dark green, light
green, dark blue, purple, white
brocade: red, pink, orange, yellow, light green, blue,
purple, white
trim: pink, yellow, light green, purple, white

WOMAN'S SHAWL ca. 1930 (*Illustrated Figure 66*)
TM 805
Loom: treadle
Pattern and Materials: ground fabric: checked plain twill
weave—wool
Colors: ground fabric: dark brown, blue, violet, white

BABY'S DIAPER SASHES ca. 1930
TM 794, 796
Loom: backstrap
Pattern and Materials: ground fabric: striped 2/2 plain
weave—cotton
Colors: ground fabric: red, orange, brown, green, dark blue,
gray (794), red, orange, brown, yellow, dark green, dark
blue (796)

BABY'S DIAPER SASH ca. 1930
TM 795
Loom: backstrap
Pattern and Materials: ground fabric: striped warp-faced
plain weave—cotton
Colors: ground fabric: orange, brown, green, dark blue,
purple

BABY'S DIAPER ca. 1930
TM 802
Loom: backstrap
Pattern and Materials: ground fabric: striped warp-faced
plain weave—cotton
Colors: ground fabric: orange, brown, yellow, dark green,
dark blue, white

■ **San Mateo Ixtatán, Huehuetenango**
HUIPIL ca. 1930
TM 714
Pattern and Materials: <u>ground fabric</u>: 1/1 plain weave, commercially milled—cotton
<u>embroidery</u>: satin, cross, buttonhole, and stem stitches—cotton, wool
Colors: <u>ground fabric</u>: white
<u>embroidery</u>: red, orange, light green, dark green

HUIPIL ca. 1930 (*Illustrated Figure 68*)
TM 713
Pattern and Materials: <u>ground fabric</u>: 1/1 plain weave, commercially milled—cotton
<u>embroidery</u>: satin, cross and overcast stitches—cotton, wool
Colors: <u>ground fabric</u>: beige
<u>embroidery</u>: red, pink, orange, yellow, green, blue, violet

■ **San Miguel Acatán, Huehuetenango**
SKIRT ca. 1930
TM 806
Loom: treadle
Pattern and Materials: <u>ground fabric</u>: solid- and *ikat*-striped 1/1 and warp-faced plain weaves—cotton
Colors: <u>ground fabric</u>: red, green, dark blue, white

■ **San Pedro Necta, Huehuetenango**
WORK *HUIPIL* ca. 1930 (*Illustrated Figure 70*)
TM 804
Loom: backstrap
Pattern and Materials: <u>ground fabric</u>: warp-faced plain weave—cotton
<u>embroidery</u>: randa, overcast and running stitches—cotton
Colors: <u>ground fabric</u>: red, white
<u>embroidery</u>: red

SKIRT ca. 1930
TM 808
Loom: backstrap
Pattern and Materials: <u>ground fabric</u>: striped warp-faced plain weave—cotton
<u>embroidery</u>: holbein, running and stem stitches—cotton
Colors: <u>ground fabric</u>: dark blue, light blue
<u>embroidery</u>: dark blue

■ **Santiago Chimaltenango, Huehuetenango**
WOMAN'S BLOUSE ca. 1930 (*Illustrated Figure 72*)
TM 1021
Loom: backstrap
Pattern and Materials: <u>ground fabric</u>: warp-faced plain weave—cotton
Colors: <u>ground fabric</u>: red, yellow, white

SKIRT ca. 1930 (*Illustrated Figure 72*)
TM 1020
Loom: treadle
Pattern and Materials: <u>ground fabric</u>: warp-faced plain weave—cotton
Colors: <u>ground fabric</u>: dark blue

WOMAN'S SASH ca. 1930 (*Illustrated Figure 72*)
TM 1022
Loom: backstrap
Pattern and Materials: <u>ground fabric</u>: striped warp-faced plain weave—wool
Colors: <u>ground fabric</u>: red, dark brown, white

WOMAN'S HEADBAND ca. 1930 (*Illustrated Figure 72*)
TM 1057
Loom: backstrap
Pattern and Materials: <u>ground fabric</u>: warp-faced plain weave—wool
Colors: <u>ground fabric</u>: red

MAN'S *TZUTE* ca. 1930 (*Illustrated Figure 73*)
TM 725
Loom: backstrap
Pattern and Materials: <u>ground fabric</u>: striped warp-faced plain weave—cotton
Colors: <u>ground fabric</u>: red, yellow

MAN'S SASH ca. 1930 (*Illustrated Figure 73*)
TM 726
Loom: backstrap
Pattern and Materials: <u>ground fabric</u>: striped weft-faced plain weave—cotton, wool
<u>brocade</u>: double-faced (interlaced weft)—cotton, wool
Colors: <u>ground fabric</u>: red
<u>brocade</u>: pink, yellow, green

MAN'S *CAPIXAY* ca. 1930 (*Illustrated Figure 73*)
TM 728
Loom: treadle
Pattern and Materials: <u>ground fabric</u>: felted plain twill weave—wool
Colors: <u>ground fabric</u>: dark brown

■ **Santa Eulalia, Huehuetenango**
SKIRT MATERIAL ca. 1930
TM 807
Loom: treadle
Pattern and Materials: <u>ground fabric</u>: solid- and *ikat*-striped 1/1 and weft-faced plain weaves—cotton
Colors: <u>ground fabric</u>: red, yellow, green, dark blue, black, white

■ **San Rafael Petzal, Huehuetenango**
HUIPIL ca. 1930 (*Illustrated Figure 74*)
TM 706

Loom: backstrap
Pattern and Materials: <u>ground fabric</u>: striped warp-faced
plain weave—cotton
<u>brocade</u>: single-faced (interlaced weft)—cotton
<u>embroidery</u>: holbein and buttonhole stitches—cotton
Colors: <u>ground fabric</u>: red, yellow, white
<u>brocade</u>: red, yellow
<u>embroidery</u>: red

■ **Todos Santos Cuchumatán, Huehuetenango**

HUIPIL ca. 1930 (*Illustrated Figure 77*)
TM 1004
Loom: backstrap
Pattern and Materials: <u>ground fabric</u>: striped 1/1 and weft-
faced plain weaves—cotton
<u>brocade</u>: single-faced (float and interlaced weft)—
cotton, wool
<u>embroidery</u>: holbein stitch—cotton
<u>trim</u>: rickrack, braiding
Colors: <u>ground fabric</u>: red, yellow, green, white
<u>brocade</u>: red, pink, orange, purple
<u>embroidery</u>: red, green
<u>trim</u>: orange, green

FIESTA HUIPIL ca. 1930
TM 711
Loom: backstrap
Pattern and Materials: <u>ground fabric</u>: striped 1/1 and warp-
faced plain weaves—cotton
<u>brocade</u>: single-faced float and weft-wrap—cotton,
wool
<u>embroidery</u>: holbein stitch—cotton
<u>trim</u>: rickrack, braiding—wool
Colors: <u>ground fabric</u>: red, yellow, green, white
<u>brocade</u>: pink, yellow, green, dark blue
<u>embroidery</u>: red, yellow, green
<u>trim</u>: blue

SKIRT ca. 1930 (*Illustrated Figure 77*)
TM 1005
Loom: treadle
Pattern and Materials: <u>ground fabric</u>: striped 2/2 plain
weave—cotton
Colors: <u>ground fabric</u>: light blue, dark blue

WOMAN'S HEADBAND ca. 1930
TM 1056
Loom: backstrap
Pattern and Materials: <u>ground fabric</u>: 2/4 and warp float
weaves—cotton, wool
Colors: <u>ground fabric</u>: red, yellow

WOMAN'S SHAWL ca. 1930
TM 671
Loom: treadle

Pattern and Materials: <u>ground fabric</u>: striped 2/2 plain
weave—cotton
Colors: <u>ground fabric</u>: light blue, dark blue

WOMAN'S SASH ca. 1930 (*Illustrated Figure 77*)
TM 1003
Loom: backstrap
Pattern and Materials: <u>ground fabric</u>: striped warp-faced
plain weave—wool
Colors: <u>ground fabric</u>: red, white, black

MAN'S SHIRT ca. 1930 (*Illustrated Figure 77*)
TM 709
Loom: backstrap
Pattern and Materials: <u>ground fabric</u>: striped 1/1 and warp-
faced weaves and plain twill weave—cotton
<u>brocade</u>: single-faced (float and interfaced weft)—
cotton, wool
Colors: <u>ground fabric</u>: red, brown, yellow, green, white
<u>brocade</u>: red, yellow, green

MAN'S TROUSERS ca. 1930 (*Illustrated Figure 77*)
TM 710
Loom: backstrap
Pattern and Materials: <u>ground fabric</u>: striped 1/1 and warp-
faced plain weaves—cotton
<u>brocade</u>: single-faced (float and interlaced weft)—
cotton
Colors: <u>ground fabric</u>: red, white
<u>brocade</u>: red, yellow, green

MAN'S SASH ca. 1930 (*Illustrated Figure 77*)
TM 708
Loom: backstrap
Pattern and Materials: <u>ground fabric</u>: plaid 2/1 and warp-
faced plain weaves—cotton
Colors: <u>ground fabric</u>: red, white

MAN'S COAT ca. 1930
TM 705
Loom: treadle
Pattern and Materials: <u>ground fabric</u>: felted plain twill
weave—cotton, wool
Colors: <u>ground fabric</u>: blue, light blue, white

MAN'S *CAPIXAY* ca. 1930
TM 703
Loom: treadle
Pattern and Materials: <u>ground fabric</u>: felted plain twill
weave—wool
Colors: <u>ground fabric</u>: black

MAN'S OVERTROUSERS ca. 1930 (*Illustrated Figure 77*)
TM 704
Loom: treadle
Pattern and Materials: <u>ground fabric</u>: felted plain twill
weave—wool

Colors: <u>ground fabric</u>: brown

MAN'S KERCHIEF ca. 1930 (*Illustrated Figure 77*)
TM 707
Pattern and Materials: <u>ground fabric</u>: 1/1 plain weave,
    commercially milled—cotton
Colors: <u>ground fabric</u>: red, white

■ **Almolonga, Quezaltenango**
FIESTA *HUIPIL* ca. 1930 (*Illustrated Figure 80*)
TM 999
Loom: backstrap
Pattern and Materials: <u>ground fabric</u>: striped 2/4, 2/1 and
    3/1 plain weaves—cotton, silk
    <u>brocade</u>: single-faced—cotton, silk
Colors: <u>ground fabric</u>: red, light orange, blue green, dark
    blue, magenta, white
    <u>brocade</u>: orange, green, purple, magenta, white

FIESTA SKIRT ca. 1930 (*Illustrated Figure 80*)
TM 1000
Loom: treadle
Pattern and Materials: <u>ground fabric</u>: solid- and *ikat*-striped
    1/1 plain weave and plain twill weave—cotton, silk
Colors: <u>ground fabric</u>: red, pink, yellow, blue, dark blue,
    white

MAN'S SHIRT ca. 1930
TM 688
Loom: backstrap
Pattern and Materials: <u>ground fabric</u>: warp-faced plain
    weave—cotton
    <u>brocade</u>: single-faced—silk
Colors: <u>ground fabric</u>: red
    <u>brocade</u>: gold, blue green, white

MAN'S SHIRT ca. 1930 (*Illustrated Figure 80*)
TM 699
Loom: backstrap
Pattern and Materials: <u>ground fabric</u>: warp-faced plain
    weave—cotton
    <u>brocade</u>: single-faced—silk
Colors: <u>ground fabric</u>: red
    <u>brocade</u>: gold, blue green, magenta, white

MAN'S SHIRT ca. 1930
TM 696
Loom: backstrap
Pattern and Materials: <u>ground fabric</u>: striped 2/2 plain
    weave—cotton
    <u>brocade</u>: single-faced—silk
Colors: <u>ground fabric</u>: red, white
    <u>brocade</u>: gold, purple, magenta

MAN'S SASH ca. 1930
TM 695

Loom: backstrap
Pattern and Materials: <u>ground fabric</u>: solid- and *ikat*-striped
    warp-faced plain weave—cotton
    <u>brocade</u>: single-faced—silk
Colors: <u>ground fabric</u>: red, dark blue, white
    <u>brocade</u>: yellow, blue green, purple, white

MAN'S "*COCHAIJ*" (SHAWL) ca. 1930
TM 690
Loom: backstrap
Pattern and Materials: <u>ground fabric</u>: warp-faced plain
    weave—cotton
    <u>brocade</u>: single-faced—silk
Colors: <u>ground fabric</u>: red
    <u>brocade</u>: orange, blue green, purple, white

MAN'S SASH ca. 1930
TM 697
Loom: backstrap
Pattern and Materials: <u>ground fabric</u>: *ikat*-striped warp-
    faced plain weave—cotton
    <u>brocade</u>: single-faced—silk
Colors: <u>ground fabric</u>: green, dark blue, white
    <u>brocade</u>: gold, purple, magenta, white

MAN'S "*COCHAIJ*" (SHAWL) ca. 1930
TM 687
Loom: backstrap
Pattern and Materials: <u>ground fabric</u>: solid- and *ikat*-striped
    2/2 plain weave—cotton
    <u>brocade</u>: single-faced float—cotton, silk
Colors: <u>ground fabric</u>: red, dark blue, white
    <u>brocade</u>: red, orange, gold, blue green, purple, magenta

■ **Concepción Chiquirichapa, Quezaltenango**
STRIP OF FABRIC ca. 1930
TM 734
Loom: backstrap
Pattern and Materials: <u>ground fabric</u>: striped 2/2 plain
    weave and plain twill weave—cotton
    <u>brocade</u>: reversal—cotton, silk
Colors: <u>ground fabric</u>: red, yellow, dark green, dark blue,
    white
    <u>brocade</u>: gold, dark green, blue green, dark blue,
    purple

WOMAN'S HEADBAND ca. 1930 (*Illustrated Figure 83*)
TM 730
Loom: backstrap
Pattern and Materials: <u>ground fabric</u>: 2/2 plain weave—
    cotton
    <u>brocade</u>: reversal—cotton, silk
Colors: <u>ground fabric</u>: dark blue
    <u>brocade</u>: yellow, blue green, purple, magenta

WOMAN'S HEADBAND ca. 1930 (*Illustrated Figure 83*)
TM 731
Loom: backstrap
Pattern and Materials: ground fabric: warp-faced plain
    weave—cotton
    brocade: reversal—silk
Colors: ground fabric: dark blue
    brocade: orange, blue green, blue, purple, magenta

SERVILLETA ca. 1930
TM 663
Loom: backstrap
Pattern and Materials: ground fabric: 3/3 plain weave—
    cotton
    brocade: reversal—cotton
Colors: ground fabric: white
    brocade: red, orange, gold, dark green, dark blue, white

TZUTE or *SERVILLETA* ca. 1930
TM 662
Loom: backstrap
Pattern and Materials: ground fabric: 2/2 plain weave—
    cotton
    brocade: reversal—cotton, silk
Colors: ground fabric: white
    brocade: red, light green, purple

SERVILLETA ca. 1930 (*Illustrated Figure 83*)
TM 724
Loom: backstrap
Pattern and Materials: ground fabric: 2/2 plain weave—
    cotton, silk
    brocade: reversal—cotton, silk
    trim: tassels—cotton, silk
Colors: ground fabric: gold, brown
    brocade: gold, magenta, white
    trim: gold, violet

MAN'S SASH ca. 1930 (*Illustrated Figure 84*)
TM 732
Loom: backstrap
Pattern and Materials: ground fabric: 2/2 plain weave—
    cotton
    brocade: reversal—cotton, silk
Colors: ground fabric: dark blue
    brocade: red, orange, blue green, magenta

MAN'S SASH ca. 1930 (*Illustrated Figure 84*)
TM 733
Loom: backstrap
Pattern and Materials: ground fabric: striped 2/3 plain
    weave—cotton
    brocade: reversal—cotton, silk
Colors: ground fabric: red
    brocade: orange, gold, dark green, blue green, dark
    blue, purple

MAN'S SASH FOR GOOD FRIDAY ca. 1930 (*Illustrated
    Figure 84*)
TM 729
Loom: backstrap
Pattern and Materials: ground fabric: warp-faced plain
    weave—cotton
    brocade: reversal—cotton, silk
Colors: ground fabric: dark blue
    brocade: orange, blue green, purple, magenta

■ **Concepción Chiquirichapa or San Juan Ostuncalco,
Quezaltenango**
TABLECLOTH ca. 1930
TM 661
Loom: backstrap
Pattern and Materials: ground fabric: 2/3 plain weave and
    horizontal ribbing—cotton
    brocade: reversal—cotton
Colors: ground fabric: white
    brocade: red, dark green

■ **San Juan Ostuncalco, Quezaltenango**
HUIPIL FABRIC ca. 1930
TM 660
Loom: treadle
Pattern and Materials: ground fabric: 2/2 plain weave—
    cotton
    brocade: reversal—cotton
Colors: ground fabric: white
    brocade: red, gold, dark green, dark blue

WEDDING HEADBAND ca. 1930
TM 669
Loom: backstrap
Pattern and Materials: ground fabric: warp-faced plain
    weave—cotton
    brocade: reversal—cotton, silk
Colors: ground fabric: dark blue
    brocade: red, orange, gold, dark green, blue green, light
    blue, purple, magenta, white

WOMAN'S SASH ca. 1930
TM 664
Loom: backstrap
Pattern and Materials: ground fabric: striped warp-faced
    plain weave and plain twill weave—cotton, silk
    brocade: reversal—cotton, silk
Colors: ground fabric: dark blue
    brocade: gold, blue green, purple, magenta

SHAWL ca. 1930
TM 666
Loom: backstrap
Pattern and Materials: ground fabric: striped 2/2 plain
    weave—cotton
Colors: ground fabric: red, yellow, dark blue, white

■ **San Martín Sacatepéquez (Chile Verde), Quezaltenango**
FIESTA *HUIPIL* ca. 1930 (*Illustrated Figure 85*)
TM 735
Loom: backstrap
Pattern and Materials: <u>ground fabric</u>: striped 2/2 and 2/3
   plain weaves—cotton
   <u>brocade</u>: reversal—cotton, silk
   <u>embroidery</u>: holbein stitch—silk
Colors: <u>ground fabric</u>: red, dark green, blue green, purple
   <u>brocade</u>: gold, blue green, purple
   <u>embroidery</u>: purple

SKIRT ca. 1930 (*Illustrated Figure 85*)
TM 736
Loom: treadle
Pattern and Materials: <u>ground fabric</u>: striped 2/2 and 3/2
   plain weaves—cotton
Colors: <u>ground fabric</u>: blue, dark blue, white

WOMAN'S SASH ca. 1930 (*Illustrated Figure 85*)
TM 727
Loom: backstrap
Pattern and Materials: <u>ground fabric</u>: striped warp-faced
   plain weave—cotton, wool
Colors: <u>ground fabric</u>: dark brown, white

■ **Quezaltenango, Quezaltenango**
HUIPIL ca. 1930 (*Illustrated Figure 91*)
TM 679
Loom: treadle
Pattern and Materials: <u>ground fabric</u>: solid- and *ikat*-striped
   1/2 and weft-faced plain weaves—cotton
   <u>brocade</u>: reversal—cotton, silk
   <u>embroidery</u>: triple buttonhole join, chain, buttonhole
   and satin stitches—cotton, silk
   <u>trim</u>: velvet—cotton
Colors: <u>ground fabric</u>: dark brown, dark blue, lavender,
   magenta, white
   <u>brocade</u>: pink, orange, light green, light blue, violet
   <u>embroidery</u>: pink, light yellow, green, purple, violet
   <u>trim</u>: black

COFRADÍA HUIPIL ca. 1930 (*Illustrated Figure 88*)
TM 674
Loom: treadle
Pattern and Materials: <u>ground fabric</u>: 1/1 and weft-faced
   plain weaves, horizontal ribbing—cotton, silk
   <u>embroidery</u>: buttonhole join, chain and buttonhole
   stitches—cotton, silk
Colors: <u>ground fabric</u>: orange, violet, white
   <u>embroidery</u>: dark red, orange, yellow, blue green, blue,
   purple, violet

MASS *HUIPIL* ca. 1930 (*Illustrated Figure 89*)
TM 675

Loom: treadle
Pattern and Materials: <u>ground fabric</u>: striped 1/1 plain
   weave—cotton, silk
   <u>brocade</u>: single-faced—cotton
   <u>embroidery</u>: buttonhole join, chain and buttonhole
   stitches—cotton, silk
Colors: <u>ground fabric</u>: yellow, purple, white
   <u>brocade</u>: white
   <u>embroidery</u>: pink, orange, yellow, light blue green,
   blue, light blue, purple, violet

FIESTA SHAWL ca. 1930
TM 672
Loom: treadle
Pattern and Materials: <u>ground fabric</u>: solid- and *ikat*-striped
   warp-faced plain weave—cotton, silk
Colors: <u>ground fabric</u>: red, orange, green, blue, dark blue,
   purple, magenta, white

SERVILLETA ca. 1930
TM 673
Loom: backstrap
Pattern and Materials: <u>ground fabric</u>: striped warp-faced,
   4/4 and 4/2 plain weaves—cotton
   <u>brocade</u>: reversal—cotton, silk
Colors: <u>ground fabric</u>: orange, white
   <u>brocade</u>: orange, purple

■ **Olintepeque, Quezaltenango**
HUIPIL ca. 1930 (*Illustrated Figure 95*)
TM 665
Loom: backstrap
Pattern and Materials: <u>ground fabric</u>: striped weft-faced
   plain weave—cotton
   <u>embroidery</u>: buttonhole join—cotton
   <u>trim</u>: ribbon—cotton
Colors: <u>ground fabric</u>: red, white
   <u>embroidery</u>: red, yellow, green
   <u>trim</u>: light blue, white

FABRIC FOR GIRL'S *HUIPIL* ca. 1930
TM 667
Loom: backstrap
Pattern and Materials: <u>ground fabric</u>: striped weft-faced and
   warp-faced plain weaves—cotton, silk
Colors: <u>ground fabric</u>: red, dark blue, magenta, white

GIRL'S SASH ca. 1930
TM 670
Loom: backstrap
Pattern and Materials: <u>ground fabric</u>: striped warp-faced
   plain weave—cotton
Colors: <u>ground fabric</u>: red, violet, white, beige

SKIRT ca. 1930
TM 668

Loom: treadle
Pattern and Materials: <u>ground fabric</u>: striped 1/1 plain weave—cotton
Colors: <u>ground fabric</u>: dark blue, white

■ **Zunil, Quezaltenango**
HUIPIL ca. 1930 (*Illustrated Figure 97*)
TM 681
Loom: backstrap
Pattern and Materials: <u>ground fabric</u>: striped 2/2 plain weave—cotton
<u>embroidery</u>: buttonhole join, buttonhole and holbein stitches—silk
Colors: <u>ground fabric</u>: blue, purple, white
<u>embroidery</u>: gold, blue green, purple, magenta

SHAWL ca. 1930 (*Illustrated Figure 97*)
TM 682
Loom: treadle
Pattern and Materials: <u>ground fabric</u>: warp-faced plain weave—cotton
Colors: <u>ground fabric</u>: dark blue, lavender, white

WOMAN'S SASH ca. 1930 (*Illustrated Figure 97*)
TM 685
Loom: backstrap
Pattern and Materials: <u>ground fabric</u>: striped weft-faced plain weave and plain twill weave—wool
Colors: <u>ground fabric</u>: red, dark brown

WOMAN'S SERVILLETA ca. 1930 (*Illustrated Figure 97*)
TM 678
Loom: backstrap
Pattern and Materials: <u>ground fabric</u>: solid- and *ikat*-striped warp-faced plain weave—cotton
Colors: <u>ground fabric</u>: brown, dark blue, violet, white

BOY'S SHIRT ca. 1930
TM 677
Loom: backstrap
Pattern and Materials: <u>ground fabric</u>: striped 2/2 and warp-faced plain weaves—cotton
<u>embroidery</u>: buttonhole stitch—cotton
Colors: <u>ground fabric</u>: red, yellow, dark green, dark blue, purple, white
<u>embroidery</u>: red, green

MAN'S SHIRT ca. 1930 (*Illustrated Figure 97*)
TM 832
Loom: backstrap
Pattern and Materials: <u>ground fabric</u>: striped 2/2 and warp-faced plain weaves—cotton
Colors: <u>ground fabric</u>: purple, white

■ **San Sebastián, Retalhuleu**
WOMAN'S HEADBAND ca. 1930
TM 838

Loom: backstrap
Pattern and Materials: <u>ground fabric</u>: warp-faced plain weave—wool
Colors: <u>ground fabric</u>: red, dark blue

■ **Magdalena Milpas Altas, Sacatepéquez**
HUIPIL ca. 1930 (*Illustrated Figure 101*)
TM 719
Loom: backstrap
Pattern and Materials: <u>ground fabric</u>: 2/2 plain weave—cotton
<u>brocade</u>: single-faced (float and weft-wrap)—cotton, silk
Colors: <u>ground fabric</u>: white
<u>brocade</u>: red, blue green, dark blue, purple

WOMAN'S SASH ca. 1930 (*Illustrated Figure 101*)
TM 723
Loom: backstrap
Pattern and Materials: <u>ground fabric</u>: warp-faced plain weave—wool
<u>embroidery</u>: satin stitch—wool, cotton, silk
<u>trim</u>: tassels—cotton, wool
Colors: <u>ground fabric</u>: white, black
<u>embroidery</u>: red, pink, orange, light yellow, green, blue, light blue, magenta
<u>trim</u>: red, pink, orange, yellow green, blue, white

WOMAN'S FIESTA *TZUTE* ca. 1930 (*Illustrated Figure 101*)
TM 721
Pattern and Materials: <u>ground fabric</u>: 1/1 plain weave, commercially milled—cotton
<u>embroidery</u>: holbein and zigzag stitches—cotton
Colors: <u>ground fabric</u>: white
<u>embroidery</u>: red, yellow, dark green, white

■ **San Antonio Aguas Calientes, Sacatepéquez**
SERVILLETA ca. 1930 (*Illustrated Figure 102*)
TM 609
Loom: backstrap
Pattern and Materials: <u>ground fabric</u>: 2/2 plain weave—cotton
<u>brocade</u>: double-faced—cotton, silk
Colors: <u>ground fabric</u>: dark blue
<u>brocade</u>: yellow, blue green, violet, magenta, white

■ **Santa María Cauque, Sacatepéquez**
HUIPIL ca. 1930 (*Illustrated Figure 104*)
TM 701
Loom: backstrap
Pattern and Materials: <u>ground fabric</u>: striped warp-faced plain weave—cotton
<u>brocade</u>: reversal—cotton, silk
<u>embroidery</u>: buttonhole and randa stitches—cotton, silk

Colors: <u>ground fabric</u>: red, white
  <u>brocade</u>: red, yellow, dark green, purple, magenta
  <u>embroidery</u>: orange, dark green, magenta

"OLD STYLE" *HUIPIL* ca. 1930 (*Illustrated Figure 106*)
TM 702
Loom: backstrap
Pattern and Materials: <u>ground fabric</u>: checked 2/2 plain
  weave—cotton
  <u>brocade</u>: reversal—cotton
Colors: <u>ground fabric</u>: red, yellow
  <u>brocade</u>: yellow, green

COFRADÍA HUIPIL ca. 1930 (*Illustrated Figure 107*)
TM 686
Loom: backstrap
Pattern and Materials: <u>ground fabric</u>: 3/3 plain weave—
  cotton
  <u>brocade</u>: reversal—cotton, silk
  <u>embroidery</u>: randa, buttonhole and overcast stitches—
  cotton, silk
Colors: <u>ground fabric</u>: white
  <u>brocade</u>: red, yellow, dark green, light blue, dark blue,
  purple, violet
  <u>embroidery</u>: red, pink, dark blue

GIRL'S *HUIPIL* ca. 1930
TM 694
Loom: backstrap
Pattern and Materials: <u>ground fabric</u>: striped 3/3 plain
  weave—cotton
  <u>brocade</u>: reversal—cotton, wool, silk
  <u>embroidery</u>: running stitch—silk
  <u>trim</u>: taffeta ribbon
Colors: <u>ground fabric</u>: red, white
  <u>brocade</u>: pink, yellow, dark green, blue, dark blue,
  purple, violet
  <u>embroidery</u>: magenta
  <u>trim</u>: pink, violet

WOMAN'S SASH ca. 1930 (*Illustrated Figure 104*)
TM 698
Loom: backstrap
Pattern and Materials: <u>ground fabric</u>: striped warp-faced
  plain weave—cotton
  <u>brocade</u>: reversal and double-faced—cotton, silk, wool
Colors: <u>ground fabric</u>: red, brown, yellow, white
  <u>brocade</u>: red, orange, dark green, blue green, purple,
  magenta

SERVILLETA ca. 1930
TM 693
Loom: backstrap
Pattern and Materials: <u>ground fabric</u>: plaid 2/2 plain
  weave—cotton

  brocade: reversal—cotton
Colors: <u>ground fabric</u>: red, dark blue
  <u>brocade</u>: orange, yellow, dark green, white

"OLD STYLE" *SERVILLETA* ca. 1930
TM 689
Loom: backstrap
Pattern and Materials: <u>ground fabric</u>: checked 2/2 plain
  weave—cotton, silk
  <u>brocade</u>: reversal—cotton
Colors: <u>ground fabric</u>: red, blue
  <u>brocade</u>: yellow, blue green, purple, magenta, white

"OLD STYLE" *SERVILLETA* ca. 1930
TM 691
Loom: backstrap
Pattern and Materials: <u>ground fabric</u>: checked 2/2 plain
  weave—cotton
  <u>brocade</u>: reversal—cotton
  <u>embroidery</u>: randa stitch—cotton, silk
Colors: <u>ground fabric</u>: red, blue
  <u>brocade</u>: orange, green, white
  <u>embroidery</u>: red, yellow, green, purple, violet

■ **Santo Domingo Xenacoj, Sacatepéquez**
HUIPIL ca. 1930 (*Illustrated Figure 108*)
TM 818
Loom: backstrap
Pattern and Materials: <u>ground fabric</u>: striped warp-faced
  plain weave—cotton
  <u>brocade</u>: reversal—cotton, silk
  <u>embroidery</u>: buttonhole and randa stitches—cotton,
  silk
Colors: <u>ground fabric</u>: red, brown, yellow
  <u>brocade</u>: yellow, blue green, purple, violet, magenta
  <u>embroidery</u>: yellow, blue green, purple, violet, magenta

COFRADÍA HUIPIL ca. 1930 (*Illustrated Figure 108*)
TM 739
Loom: backstrap
Pattern and Materials: <u>ground fabric</u>: striped 2/2, 2/3 and
  warp-faced plain weaves—cotton
  <u>brocade</u>: reversal—cotton, silk
  <u>embroidery</u>: buttonhole and randa stitches—cotton,
  silk
Colors: <u>ground fabric</u>: red, white
  <u>brocade</u>: red, purple, violet, magenta
  <u>embroidery</u>: blue green, purple, violet, magenta

HUIPIL ca. 1930
TM 820
Loom: backstrap
Pattern and Materials: <u>ground fabric</u>: striped warp-faced
  plain weave—cotton
  <u>embroidery</u>: holbein, randa and buttonhole stitches—
  cotton, silk

Colors: <u>ground fabric</u>: red, brown, yellow
    <u>embroidery</u>: red, purple, magenta
SKIRT ca. 1930
TM 819
Loom: treadle
Pattern and Materials: <u>ground fabric</u>: 2/2 plain weave—
    cotton
Colors: <u>ground fabric</u>: dark blue

COFRADÍA SERVILLETA ca. 1930
TM 827
Loom: backstrap
Pattern and Materials: <u>ground fabric</u>: striped 3/3 and warp-
    faced plain weaves—cotton
    <u>brocade</u>: reversal—cotton
Colors: <u>ground fabric</u>: white
    <u>brocade</u>: red, tan

SERVILLETA ca. 1930
TM 742
Loom: backstrap
Pattern and Materials: <u>ground fabric</u>: 3/3 and warp-faced
    plain weaves—cotton, silk
    <u>brocade</u>: reversal—cotton, silk
Colors: <u>ground fabric</u>: red, yellow
    <u>brocade</u>: yellow, blue green, purple, violet, magenta,
    white

SERVILLETA ca. 1930
TM 740
Loom: backstrap
Pattern and Materials: <u>ground fabric</u>: warp-faced plain
    weave—cotton
    <u>brocade</u>: reversal—cotton, silk
Colors: <u>ground fabric</u>: red
    <u>brocade</u>: yellow, blue green, purple, violet, magenta,
    white, black

WOMAN'S *TZUTE* ca. 1930
TM 810
Loom: backstrap
Pattern and Materials: <u>ground fabric</u>: 3/2 plain weave—
    cotton
    <u>brocade</u>: single-faced and reversal—cotton, silk
Colors: <u>ground fabric</u>: white
    <u>brocade</u>: red, orange, green, blue green, blue, dark
    <u>blue</u>, purple, magenta

■ **Sumpango, Sacatepéquez**
WORK *HUIPIL* OR INSIDE *HUIPIL* ca. 1930
TM 987
Loom: backstrap
Pattern and Materials: <u>ground fabric</u>: 2/2 plain weave—
    cotton

    <u>embroidery</u>: buttonhole stitch—silk
Colors: <u>ground fabric</u>: white
    <u>embroidery</u>: blue green, purple, magenta

TOP *HUIPIL* ca. 1930 (*Illustrated Figure 110*)
TM 991
Loom: backstrap
Pattern and Materials: <u>ground fabric</u>: striped warp-faced
    plain weave—cotton, silk
    <u>embroidery</u>: satin, chain, closed herringbone, randa,
    and buttonhole stitches—silk
Colors: <u>ground fabric</u>: red, tan, blue green, purple
    <u>embroidery</u>: pink, blue green, light blue, purple,
    magenta, white

SKIRT ca. 1930 (*Illustrated Figure 110*)
TM 990
Loom: treadle
Pattern and Materials: <u>ground fabric</u>: 2/2 plain weave—
    cotton
    <u>embroidery</u>: randa stitch—silk
Colors: <u>ground fabric</u>: dark blue
    <u>embroidery</u>: blue green, purple, violet

WOMAN'S SASH ca. 1930 (*Illustrated Figure 110*)
TM 992
Loom: backstrap
Pattern and Materials: <u>ground fabric</u>: striped warp-faced
    plain weave—cotton
    <u>brocade</u>: reversal—cotton, silk
Colors: <u>ground fabric</u>: pink, yellow, dark green, dark blue,
    purple, white
    <u>brocade</u>: pink, orange, blue green, blue, purple,
    magenta, white

WOMAN'S HAIR TIE ca. 1930 (*Illustrated Figure 110*)
TM 1055
Loom: backstrap
Pattern and Materials: <u>ground fabric</u>: weft-faced plain
    weave—cotton, silk, wool
Colors: <u>ground fabric</u>: red, yellow, blue green, light blue,
    magenta, white, black

■ **San Marcos, San Marcos**
HUIPIL ca. 1930 (*Illustrated Figure 111*)
TM 650
Loom: backstrap
Pattern and Materials: <u>ground fabric</u>: 1/1 and 2/2 plain
    weaves and plain twill weave—cotton
    <u>brocade</u>: reversal—cotton, silk
    <u>trim</u>: cotton velvet
Colors: <u>ground fabric</u>: white
    <u>brocade</u>: yellow, violet
    <u>trim</u>: black

HUIPIL FABRIC ca. 1930

TM 651
Loom: backstrap
Pattern and Materials: <u>ground fabric</u>: 2/2 plain weave—
    cotton
    <u>brocade</u>: reversal—cotton
Colors: <u>ground fabric</u>: white
    <u>brocade</u>: yellow, blue gray

■ **San Pedro Sacatepéquez, San Marcos**
SKIRT FABRIC ca. 1930 (*Illustrated Figure 113*)
TM 648
Loom: treadle
Pattern and Materials: <u>ground fabric</u>: plain- and *ikat*-
    striped 1/1 and 1/2 plain weaves—cotton
Colors: <u>ground fabric</u>: gold, yellow, dark blue, white

■ **Santa Catarina Nahualá, Sololá**
WORK *HUIPIL* ca. 1930
TM 658
Loom: backstrap
Pattern and Materials: <u>ground fabric</u>: warp-faced plain
    weave—cotton
    <u>embroidery</u>: holbein, backstitch and buttonhole join
    stitches—rayon
Colors: <u>ground fabric</u>: white
    <u>embroidery</u>: red

MASS *HUIPIL* ca. 1930 (*Illustrated Figure 114*)
TM 998
Loom: backstrap
Pattern and Materials: <u>ground fabric</u>: warp-faced plain
    weave—cotton
    <u>brocade</u>: reversal—cotton, silk, rayon, wool
    <u>embroidery</u>: holbein and backstitch stitches—rayon
Colors: <u>ground fabric</u>: white
    <u>brocade</u>: red, orange, yellow, dark green, blue green,
    blue, magenta, black
    <u>embroidery</u>: magenta

SKIRT ca. 1930
TM 997
Loom: treadle
Pattern and Materials: <u>ground fabric</u>: striped 2/2 plain
    weave—cotton
    <u>embroidery</u>: buttonhole join—silk
Colors: <u>ground fabric</u>: dark blue, white
    <u>embroidery</u>: yellow, blue green, purple, violet

WOMAN'S SASH ca. 1930
TM 996
Loom: backstrap
Pattern and Materials: <u>ground fabric</u>: striped warp-faced
    plain weave—cotton
    <u>brocade</u>: reversal—silk
    <u>embroidery</u>: cross-stitch—silk

Colors: <u>ground fabric</u>: pink, dark blue
    <u>brocade</u>: orange, yellow, green, blue green, magenta,
    white
    <u>embroidery</u>: orange, yellow, blue green, light blue,
    magenta

WOMAN'S *TZUTE* ca. 1930
TM 656
Loom: backstrap
Pattern and Materials: <u>ground fabric</u>: striped warp-faced
    and 2/2 plain weaves—cotton
Colors: <u>ground fabric</u>: red, orange, tan, yellow, dark green,
    white, black

WOMAN'S *TZUTE* ca. 1930
TM 654
Loom: backstrap
Pattern and Materials: <u>ground fabric</u>: striped warp-faced
    and 2/2 plain weaves—cotton
    <u>embroidery</u>: holbein stitch—cotton
Colors: <u>ground fabric</u>: red, brown, dark blue, white
    <u>embroidery</u>: red

MAN'S SHIRT ca. 1930 (*Illustrated Figure 116*)
TM 985
Loom: backstrap
Pattern and Materials: <u>ground fabric</u>: striped warp-faced
    and 2/2 plain weaves—cotton
    <u>brocade</u>: reversal—silk, rayon
    <u>embroidery</u>: holbein, running and backstitch stitches—
    silk
Colors: <u>ground fabric</u>: red, orange, yellow, dark blue, white
    <u>brocade</u>: pink, orange
    <u>embroidery</u>: pink, magenta

TROUSERS ca. 1930 (*Illustrated Figure 116*)
TM 989
Loom: backstrap
Pattern and Materials: <u>ground fabric</u>: warp-faced plain
    weave—cotton
    <u>brocade</u>: reversal—silk
    <u>embroidery</u>: backstitch—silk
Colors: <u>ground fabric</u>: white
    <u>brocade</u>: red, yellow
    <u>embroidery</u>: pink

MAN'S SASH ca. 1930 (*Illustrated Figure 116*)
TM 983
Loom: backstrap
Pattern and Materials: <u>ground fabric</u>: warp-faced plain
    weave—cotton, silk
    <u>brocade</u>: reversal—silk, rayon
Colors: <u>ground fabric</u>: pink, dark blue, magenta
    <u>brocade</u>: pink, orange, yellow, magenta

JACKET ca. 1930

TM 988
Loom: treadle
Pattern and Materials: ground fabric: felted plain twill
    weave—wool
Colors: ground fabric: dark brown

MAN'S NECKERCHIEF ca. 1930 (*Illustrated Figure 116*)
TM 984
Loom: treadle
Pattern and Materials: ground fabric: striped warp-faced
    plain weave—cotton
    brocade: reversal—silk
Colors: ground fabric: red, yellow, dark green, white
    brocade: orange, yellow, blue green, magenta

MAN'S APRON ca. 1930 (*Illustrated Figure 116*)
TM 986
Loom: treadle
Pattern and Materials: ground fabric: checked and felted
    plain twill weave—wool
Colors: ground fabric: dark brown, white

■ **Panajachel, Sololá**
FIESTA *HUIPIL* ca. 1930 (*Illustrated Figure 118*)
TM 640
Loom: backstrap
Pattern and Materials: ground fabric: striped warp-faced
    plain weave—cotton
    brocade: reversal—silk
    embroidery: stem and overcast stitches—silk
Colors: ground fabric: red, tan
    brocade: purple
    embroidery: purple

FIESTA *HUIPIL* ca. 1930
TM 643
Loom: backstrap
Pattern and Materials: ground fabric: striped warp-faced
    plain weave—cotton
    brocade: reversal and single-faced (wrap)—cotton, silk
    embroidery: overcast stitch—silk
Colors: ground fabric: red, brown, white
    brocade: red, yellow, green, blue green, blue, magenta,
    purple, white
    embroidery: magenta

SKIRT ca. 1930 (*Illustrated Figure 118*)
TM 637
Loom: treadle
Pattern and Materials: ground fabric: 2/2 plain weave—
    cotton
    embroidery: buttonhole join—silk
Colors: ground fabric: dark blue
    embroidery: purple, white

WOMAN'S SASH ca. 1930 (*Illustrated Figure 118*)

TM 629
Loom: backstrap
Pattern and Materials: ground fabric: plain- and *ikat*-
    striped warp-faced plain weave—cotton
    brocade: double-faced—silk
Colors: ground fabric: red, yellow, dark green, dark blue,
    violet, white
    brocade: orange, blue green, purple, magenta, white

WOMAN'S HAIR TIE ca. 1930
TM 835
Loom: backstrap
Pattern and Materials: ground fabric: double-faced warp
    float weave—cotton, wool
Colors: ground fabric: red, dark blue, white

WOMAN'S *TZUTE* ca. 1930 (*Illustrated Figure 118*)
TM 633
Loom: backstrap
Pattern and Materials: ground fabric: plain- and *ikat*-
    striped warp-faced plain weave—cotton
    brocade: single-faced (wrap)—cotton, silk
Colors: ground fabric: red, orange, yellow, dark blue, violet,
    white
    brocade: yellow, blue green, purple, magenta, white

■ **San Andrés Semetabaj, Sololá**
HUIPIL ca. 1930 (*Illustrated Figure 120*)
TM 981
Loom: backstrap
Pattern and Materials: ground fabric: striped 2/2 plain
    weave—cotton
    brocade: reversal and single-faced (weft-wrap)—cotton,
    wool, silk
Colors: ground fabric: dark blue, white
    brocade: red, dark green, dark blue

SKIRT FABRIC ca. 1930 (*Illustrated Figure 120*)
TM 982
Loom: treadle
Pattern and Materials: ground fabric: checked 1/1 plain
    weave—cotton
Colors: ground fabric: red, dark blue, white

WOMAN'S SASH ca. 1930 (*Illustrated Figure 120*)
TM 980
Loom: backstrap
Pattern and Materials: ground fabric: warp-faced plain
    weave—cotton
    brocade: single-faced—cotton, wool
Colors: ground fabric: dark green, dark blue, white
    brocade: red, pink, orange, yellow, dark green, dark
    blue

WOMAN'S *SERVILLETA* ca. 1930 (*Illustrated Figure 120*)
TM 632

Loom: backstrap
Pattern and Materials: <u>ground fabric</u>: striped warp-faced plain weave—cotton
<u>brocade</u>: reversal and single-faced (float and weft-wrap)—cotton, wool
Colors: <u>ground fabric</u>: white
<u>brocade</u>: red, pink, dark green, dark blue

SERVILLETA ca. 1930 (*Illustrated Figure 120*)
TM 630
Loom: backstrap
Pattern and Materials: <u>ground fabric</u>: plaid 2/2 plain weave—cotton
Colors: <u>ground fabric</u>: red, dark blue, white

■ **San Lucas Tolimán, Sololá**
HUIPIL FABRIC ca. 1930 (*Illustrated Figure 124*)
TM 639
Loom: backstrap
Pattern and Materials: <u>ground fabric</u>: warp-faced plain weave—cotton
<u>brocade</u>: single-faced (float and soumak)—cotton
Colors: <u>ground fabric</u>: dark blue
<u>brocade</u>: red, yellow, blue, gray, purple

■ **San Marcos la Laguna, Sololá**
HUIPIL ca. 1930 (*Illustrated Figure 130*)
TM 979
Loom: backstrap
Pattern and Materials: <u>ground fabric</u>: striped warp-faced plain weave—cotton
Colors: <u>ground fabric</u>: red, yellow, dark green, white

TZUTE ca. 1930
TM 627
Loom: backstrap
Pattern and Materials: <u>ground fabric</u>: striped warp-faced plain weave—cotton
<u>embroidery</u>: chain stitch—cotton
Colors: <u>ground fabric</u>: red, pink, orange, purple, white
<u>embroidery</u>: pink, purple

■ **Santa Cruz la Laguna, Sololá**
MAN'S HEADKERCHIEF ca. 1930
TM 1015
Loom: backstrap
Pattern and Materials: <u>ground fabric</u>: striped warp-faced plain weave—cotton
Colors: <u>ground fabric</u>: red, orange, dark green, white

■ **Santa Lucía Utatlán, Sololá**
SERVILLETA ca. 1930
TM 788
Loom: backstrap
Pattern and Materials: <u>ground fabric</u>: 1/1 and weft-faced plain weaves, horizontal ribbing—cotton

<u>brocade</u>: reversal—cotton, silk
Colors: <u>ground fabric</u>: white
<u>brocade</u>: red, gold, dark green, light blue

SERVILLETA ca. 1930 (*Illustrated Figure 131*)
TM 789
Loom: backstrap
Pattern and Materials: <u>ground fabric</u>: 2/2 and weft-faced plain weaves—cotton
<u>brocade</u>: reversal—cotton, silk
Colors: <u>ground fabric</u>: white
<u>brocade</u>: red, pink, yellow, dark green, blue green, dark blue, purple, violet

■ **Santiago Atitlán, Sololá**
HUIPIL ca. 1930 (*Illustrated Figure 132*)
TM 1017
Loom: backstrap
Pattern and Materials: <u>ground fabric</u>: striped warp-faced plain weave—cotton
<u>brocade</u>: single-faced (float and weft-wrap)—cotton, silk
<u>embroidery</u>: stem and closed herringbone stitches—cotton, silk
Colors: <u>ground fabric</u>: orange, violet, white
<u>brocade</u>: orange, green, violet, magenta
<u>embroidery</u>: orange, green, violet, magenta
<u>trim</u>: pink

SKIRT ca. 1930 (*Illustrated Figure 132*)
TM 1016
Loom: treadle
Pattern and Materials: <u>ground fabric</u>: plain- and *ikat*-striped 1/1 plain weave—cotton
Colors: <u>ground fabric</u>: red, dark blue, white

SHIRT ca. 1930 (*Illustrated Figure 136*)
TM 1038
Loom: backstrap
Pattern and Materials: <u>ground fabric</u>: warp-faced plain weave—cotton
Colors: <u>ground fabric</u>: red, orange, dark green, dark blue, violet

TROUSERS ca. 1930
TM 1036
Loom: backstrap
Pattern and Materials: <u>ground fabric</u>: striped warp-faced plain weave—cotton
<u>brocade</u>: single-faced (float and weft-wrap)—cotton, silk
Colors: <u>ground fabric</u>: orange, purple, white
<u>brocade</u>: orange, green, violet, magenta

TROUSERS ca. 1930
TM 642

Loom: backstrap
Pattern and Materials: <u>ground fabric</u>: striped warp-faced
  plain weave—cotton
  <u>brocade</u>: single-faced (float and weft-wrap)—cotton,
  silk
Colors: <u>ground fabric</u>: orange, purple, white
  <u>brocade</u>: orange, green, violet, magenta

BOY'S TROUSERS ca. 1930
TM 631
Loom: backstrap
Pattern and Materials: <u>ground fabric</u>: striped warp-faced
  plain weave—cotton
  <u>brocade</u>: single-faced (float and weft-wrap)—cotton,
  silk
Colors: <u>ground fabric</u>: orange, violet, magenta, white
  <u>brocade</u>: orange, green, violet, magenta

MAN'S SASH ca. 1930 (*Illustrated Figure 136*)
TM 1037
Loom: backstrap
Pattern and Materials: <u>ground fabric</u>: striped warp-faced
  plain weave—cotton
Colors: <u>ground fabric</u>: red, dark blue

MAN'S SASH ca. 1930
TM 634
Loom: backstrap
Pattern and Materials: <u>ground fabric</u>: striped warp-faced
  plain weave—cotton
Colors: <u>ground fabric</u>: red, dark blue, violet

MAN'S HATBAND *TZUTE* ca. 1930 (*Illustrated Figure 136*)
TM 1039
Loom: backstrap
Pattern and Materials: <u>ground fabric</u>: striped warp-faced
  plain weave—cotton, silk
Colors: <u>ground fabric</u>: red, orange, brown, violet

■ **Sololá, Sololá**
WEDDING *HUIPIL* ca. 1930 (*Illustrated Figure 137*)
TM 635
Loom: backstrap
Pattern and Materials: <u>ground fabric</u>: striped warp-faced
  and 2/2 plain weaves—cotton
  <u>brocade</u>: single-faced (weft-wrap)—cotton, silk
  <u>embroidery</u>: running, stem and buttonhole join
  stitches—cotton, silk
  <u>trim</u>: silk cloth
Colors: <u>ground fabric</u>: red, yellow, green, white
  <u>brocade</u>: yellow, green, violet, white
  <u>embroidery</u>: red, pink, white
  <u>trim</u>: pink

WOMAN'S SHIRT ca. 1930 (*Illustrated Figure 137*)
TM 638

Loom: backstrap
Pattern and Materials: <u>ground fabric</u>: plain- and *ikat*-
  striped warp-faced plain weave—cotton
  <u>brocade</u>: double-faced—silk
  <u>embroidery</u>: stem and backstitch stitches—silk
Colors: <u>ground fabric</u>: red, yellow, dark green, dark blue,
  white
  <u>brocade</u>: yellow, blue green, purple, magenta, white
  <u>embroidery</u>: blue green, light blue, magenta, white

SKIRT ca. 1930
TM 636
Loom: treadle
Pattern and Materials: <u>ground fabric</u>: striped 2/2 plain
  weave—cotton
  <u>embroidery</u>: buttonhole join—silk
Colors: <u>ground fabric</u>: dark blue, white
  <u>embroidery</u>: gold, purple

WOMAN'S SHIRT ca. 1930
TM 995
Loom: backstrap
Pattern and Materials: <u>ground fabric</u>: plain- and *ikat*-
  striped warp-faced plain weave—cotton
  <u>embroidery</u>: backstitch—silk
Colors: <u>ground fabric</u>: red, pink, orange, dark blue, violet,
  white
  <u>embroidery</u>: yellow, green, purple, magenta

TROUSERS ca. 1930
TM 994
Loom: backstrap
Pattern and Materials: <u>ground fabric</u>: striped warp-faced
  plain weave—cotton, silk
Colors: <u>ground fabric</u>: red, orange, green, dark green,
  purple, magenta, white

MAN'S *TZUTE* ca. 1930
TM 641
Loom: backstrap
Pattern and Materials: <u>ground fabric</u>: striped warp-faced
  plain weave—cotton
  <u>embroidery</u>: buttonhole join—silk
Colors: <u>ground fabric</u>: red, yellow, dark green, dark blue,
  violet, white
  <u>embroidery</u>: yellow, green, purple, magenta, white

MAN'S BAG ca. 1930
TM 993
Pattern and Materials: <u>ground fabric</u>: knitted-wool
Colors: <u>ground fabric</u>: dark brown, white

■ **Momostenango, Totonicapán**
MAN'S SASH ca. 1930 (*Illustrated Figure 140*)
TM 756
Loom: treadle

Pattern and Materials: ground fabric: plain twill weave—wool

Colors: ground fabric: pink, brown, light blue, white, black

■ **San Cristóbal Totonicapán, Totonicapán**

WOMAN'S COLLAR (GOLA) for HUIPIL ca. 1930 (Illustrated Figure 141)

TM 1011

Pattern and Materials: ground fabric: 1/1 and 2/2 plain weaves, commercially milled—cotton
embroidery: cross and chain stitches—silk
trim: lace—silk

Colors: ground fabric: beige
embroidery: pink, orange, yellow, blue green, blue, purple, magenta
trim: dark red, pink, blue green, blue

WOMAN'S SHAWL ca. 1930

TM 752

Loom: treadle

Pattern and Materials: ground fabric: striped warp-faced plain weave—cotton

Colors: ground fabric: orange, dark green, dark blue, white

WOMAN'S SHAWL OR SKIRT FABRIC ca. 1930

TM 1014

Loom: treadle

Pattern and Materials: ground fabric: plain- and ikat-striped 2/2 plain weave—cotton

Colors: ground fabric: yellow, green, blue, dark blue, purple, white

WOMAN'S HAIR TIE ca. 1930

TM 757

Loom: small treadle (cf. O'Neale 1945, p. 37 and Figure 19h)

Pattern and Materials: ground fabric: striped weft-faced plain weave—cotton, silk
trim: tassels, pompons (silk), wire-wrapped maguey fiber loops

Colors: ground fabric: red, pink, yellow, blue green, blue, violet, white, black
trim: red, yellow, blue green, blue, purple, white

WOMAN'S HAIR TIE ca. 1930

TM 1019

Loom: backstrap

Pattern and Materials: ground fabric: striped weft-faced plain weave—cotton, wool, silk

Colors: ground fabric: red, pink, yellow, green, violet, white, black

■ **Santa María Chiquimula, Totonicapán**

HUIPIL ca. 1930 (Illustrated Figure 142)

TM 659

Loom: backstrap

Pattern and Materials: ground fabric: striped warp-faced plain weave—cotton
embroidery: stem, holbein and buttonhole join stitches—silk

Colors: ground fabric: red, dark blue
embroidery: orange, magenta

HUIPIL ca. 1930

TM 652

Loom: backstrap

Pattern and Materials: ground fabric: striped warp-faced plain weave—cotton
embroidery: randa, holbein and buttonhole join stitches—silk

Colors: ground fabric: red, dark blue, white
embroidery: orange, gold, magenta

SKIRT ca. 1930

TM 657

Loom: treadle

Pattern and Materials: ground fabric: 1/1 plain weave—cotton
embroidery: running and buttonhole join stitches—silk

Colors: ground fabric: dark blue, white
embroidery: yellow, purple, violet

WOMAN'S HEADDRESS (TOCOYAL) ca. 1930 (Illustrated Figure 142)

TM 837

Pattern and Materials: ground fabric: braided—cotton
trim: tassels—cotton

Colors: ground fabric: dark blue
trim: dark blue

WOMAN'S TZUTE or SHAWL ca. 1930 (Illustrated Figure 142)

TM 655

Loom: backstrap

Pattern and Materials: ground fabric: striped warp-faced plain weave—cotton
embroidery: buttonhole, holbein and buttonhole join stitches—silk

Colors: ground fabric: dark blue, white
embroidery: orange, gold, purple, magenta

■ **Totonicapán, Totonicapán**

MASS HUIPIL ca. 1930 (Illustrated Figure 147)

TM 1013

Loom: backstrap

Pattern and Materials: ground fabric: 1/1 plain weave—cotton
brocade: single-faced—cotton
trim: silk cloth

Colors: ground fabric: white
brocade: white
trim: violet

MASS *HUIPIL* ca. 1930 (*Illustrated Figure 146*)
TM 746
Pattern and Materials: ground fabric: commercial lace net with machine-stitched embroidery—cotton
embroidery: chain and satin stitches—silk
trim: lace (silk), ribbon (velvet), sequins (metal)
Colors: ground fabric: white
embroidery: red, pink, yellow, blue green, blue, purple
trim: pink, blue (lace), pink (ribbon), gold (sequins)

COFRADÍA HUIPIL ca. 1930
TM 751
Loom: backstrap
Pattern and Materials: ground fabric: 1/1 plain weave—cotton
brocade: single-faced—cotton
Colors: ground fabric: white
brocade: white

MASS VEIL ca. 1930
TM 747
Pattern and Materials: ground fabric: commercial lace net with machine-stitched embroidery—cotton
Colors: ground fabric: white

MASS VEIL ca. 1930
TM 749
Loom: backstrap
Pattern and Materials: ground fabric: 1/1 plain weave—cotton
brocade: single-faced—cotton
Colors: ground fabric: white
brocade: white

WOMAN'S SASH ca. 1930 (*Illustrated Figure 148*)
TM 755
Loom: backstrap
Pattern and Materials: ground fabric: warp-faced plain weave and warp-faced float weave—cotton
brocade: single-faced—silk
Colors: ground fabric: white, black
brocade: red, orange, blue green, purple, black

WOMAN'S SASH ca. 1930 (*Illustrated Figure 148*)
TM 1012
Loom: backstrap
Pattern and Materials: ground fabric: warp-faced plain weave and warp-faced float weave—cotton
brocade: single-faced—silk
Colors: ground fabric: dark blue, white
brocade: pink, dark brown, yellow, blue green, purple, magenta

FIESTA HAIR TIE ca. 1930 (*Illustrated Figure 148*)
TM 1018
Loom: small treadle (cf. O'Neale 1945, p. 37 and Figure 19h)
Pattern and Materials: ground fabric: weft-faced (slit tapestry) plain weave—cotton, silk
trim: tassels, pompons (silk) and wire-wrapped maguey fiber loops
Colors: ground fabric: gold, blue green, light blue, purple, magenta, white, black
trim: blue green, magenta

SERVILLETA ca. 1930
TM 750
Loom: backstrap
Pattern and Materials: ground fabric: solid- and *ikat*-striped weft-faced plain weave—cotton
Colors: ground fabric: red, orange, yellow, dark blue, white, black

SERVILLETA ca. 1930
TM 748
Loom: backstrap
Pattern and Materials: ground fabric: weft-faced plain weave—cotton
Colors: ground fabric: red, brown, yellow, dark green, white, black

FIESTA SKIRT ca. 1930 (*Illustrated Figure 147*)
TM 649
Loom: treadle
Pattern and Materials: ground fabric: plain- and *ikat*-striped 1/1 plain weave—cotton, silk
trim: ribbon—silk
Colors: ground fabric: red, yellow, dark blue, white
trim: green

INDEX OF FIGURES

Bibliography

Adams, Richard N.
  1970   *Crucifixion by Power: Essays on Guatemalan National Social Structure, 1944-1966.* Austin: University of Texas Press.
Anawalt, Patricia
  1977   "Suggestions for Methodological Approaches to the Study of Costume Change in Middle American Indigenous Dress." In *Ethnographic Textiles of the Western Hemisphere: Irene Emery Roundtable on Museum Textiles, 1976 Proceedings,* edited by Irene Emery and Patricia Fiske, pp. 106-122. Washington, D.C.: The Textile Museum.
Anderson, Marilyn
  1978   *Guatemalan Textiles Today.* New York: Watson-Guptill Publications.
Bjerregaard, Lena
  1977a   *The Techniques of Guatemalan Backstrap Weaving.* New York: Van Nostrand Reinhold Co.
  1977b   "Recent Changes of Pattern in Guatemalan Backstrap Weaving." In *Ethnographic Textiles of the Western Hemisphere: Irene Emery Roundtable on Museum Textiles, 1976 Proceedings,* edited by Irene Emery and Patricia Fiske, pp. 133-142. Washington, D.C.: The Textile Museum.
Breuer, Alice P.
  1942   *Guatemalan Textiles: The Prentiss N. Gray Collection.* Oakland, Calif.: Mills College.
Bunch, Roland, and Roger Bunch
  1977   *The Highland Maya: Patterns of Life and Clothing in Indian Guatemala.* Visalia, Calif.: Indigenous Publications.
Bunzel, Ruth
  1952   *Chichicastenango: A Guatemalan Village.* Publications of the American Ethnological Society, 22. Locust Valley, N.Y.: J. J. Augustin.
Carmack, Robert M.
  1976   "Estratificacion y Cambio Social en las Terras Altas Occidentales de Guatemala: el Caso de Tecpanaco." *America Indigena* 36:253-301.
  1981   *The Quiché Mayas of Utatlán: The Evolution of a Highland Guatemalan Kingdom.* Norman: University of Oklahoma Press.
Coe, Michael
  1966   *The Maya.* London: Thames & Hudson.
  1977   *Mexico.* New York: Praeger.
Colby, Benjamin N., and Pierre Van Den Berghe
  1969   *Ixil Country: A Plural Society in Highland Guatemala.* Berkeley: University of California Press.
Conte, Christine
  1974   "Traditional Craft Production in Two Quichean Municipios of Highland Guatemala." Unpublished manuscript. Albany: State University of New York.
  1975   "Guatemalan Archeology: A Synthesis." Unpublished manuscript. Tucson: University of Arizona.
Cordry, Donald, and Dorothy Cordry
  1973   *Mexican Indian Costumes.* Austin: University of Texas Press.
Delgado, Hildegard Schmidt de
  1963   "Aboriginal Guatemalan Handweaving and Costume." Ph.D. dissertation, Indiana University. Ann Arbor: University Microfilms, 1975.
Diccionario Geográfico de Guatemala, Tomo I. Guatemala City: Direccion General de Cartografía, 1961.
Diccionario Geográfico de Guatemala, Tomo II. Guatemala City: Direccion General de Cartografía, 1962.
Dietrich, Mary G., Jon T. Erickson and Erin Younger
  1979   *Guatemalan Costumes: The Heard Museum Collection.* Phoenix: The Heard Museum.
Donnan, Christopher B., and George R. Ellis
  1975   *Guatemala: Quetzal and Cross.* Los Angeles: Frederick S. Wright Art Galleries and the University of California Press.

Edmonson, M.
  1971   *The Book of Counsel: The Popol Vuh of the Quiche Maya of Guatemala.* Middle American Research Institute Publication no. 35. New Orleans: Tulane University.
Emery, Irene
  1966   *The Primary Structures of Fabrics: An Illustrated Classification.* Washington, D.C.: The Textile Museum.
Fergusson, Erna
  1942   *Guatemala.* New York: Alfred A. Knopf.
Foster, George
  1960   *Culture and Conquest: America's Spanish Heritage.* Chicago: Quadrangle Books.
Fox, John W.
  1978   *Quiche Conquest: Centralism and Regionalism in Highland Guatemalan State Development.* Albuquerque: University of New Mexico Press.
Gruhn, Ruth
  1969   *An Introduction to Chichicastenango.* Alberta: University of Alberta.
Guatemala Scholars Network
  1981   *Guatemala Newsletter.*
Hinshaw, Robert E.
  1975   *Panajáchel: A Guatemalan Town in Thirty Year Perspective.* Pittsburgh: University of Pittsburgh Press.
Jones, Chester L.
  1940   *Guatemala, Past and Present.* Minneapolis: University of Minnesota Press.
LaFarge, Oliver
  1947   *Santa Eulalia: The Religion of a Cuchumatan Indian Town.* Chicago: University of Chicago Press.
Lambert, Anne M.
  1978   "Textile Transposal: Guatemala and North America." In *Ethnographic Textiles of the Western Hemisphere: Irene Emery Roundtable on Museum Textiles, 1976 Proceedings,* edited by Irene Emery and Patricia Fiske, pp. 143-153. Washington, D.C.: The Textile Museum.
Lathbury, Virginia
  1974   "Textiles as Expression of an Expanding World View: San Antonio Aguas Calientes, Guatemala." Master's thesis, University of Pennsylvania.
Lehmann, Henri
  1961   "Exposition Costumes Maya d'Aujourd'Hui." In *Objets et Mondes: La Revue de Musée de l'Homme* 1:1. Paris: Musée de l'Homme.
McBryde, F. W.
  1947   *Cultural and Historical Geography of Southwest Guatemala.* Institute of Social Anthropology Publication no. 4. Washington, D.C.: Smithsonian Institution Press.
Marqusee, Stephen J.
  1980   "An Analysis of Late Post Classic Period Quichean Art from the Highlands of Guatemala." Ph.D. dissertation, State University of New York at Albany.
Nash, Manning
  1967   *Machine Age Maya.* Chicago: University of Chicago Press.
  1969   "The Guatemalan Highlands." In *Handbook of Middle American Indians,* edited by Robert Wauchope, Vol. 7, pp. 30-45. Austin: University of Texas Press.
O'Neale, Lila M.
  1945   *Textiles of Highland Guatemala.* Carnegie Institution of Washington Publication no. 567. Washington, D.C.: Carnegie Institution.
Osborne, Lilly de Jongh
  1935   *Guatemalan Textiles.* Middle American Research Series Publication no. 6. New Orleans: Tulane University.
  1965   *Indian Crafts of Guatemala and El Salvador.* Norman: University of Oklahoma Press.
Pang, Hilda Delgado
  1977a   "Guatemalan Ethnographic Textiles: Background Data and State of the Art." In *Ethnographic Textiles of the Western Hemisphere: Irene Emery Roundtable on Museum Textiles, 1976 Proceedings,* edited by Irene Emery and Patricia Fiske, pp. 89-93. Washington, D.C.: The Textile Museum.

1977b   "Similarities Between Certain Early Spanish, Contemporary Spanish Folk, and Mesoamerican Indian Textile Design Motifs." In *Ethnographic Textiles of the Western Hemisphere: Irene Emery Roundtable on Museum Textiles, 1976 Proceedings*, edited by Irene Emery and Patricia Fiske, pp. 386-404. Washington, D.C.: The Textile Museum.

Pettersen, Carmen L.
1976   *The Maya of Guatemala: Their Life and Dress*. Guatemala City: Ixchel Museum.

Proskouriakoff, Tatiana
1961   "Women in Maya Art." In *Essays in Pre-Columbian Art and Archaeology* by Samuel K. Lothrop and others. Cambridge, Mass.: Harvard University Press.

Reina, Ruben E.
1969   "Eastern Guatemalan Highlands: The Pokomames and Chorti." In *Handbook of Middle American Indians*, edited by Robert Wauchope, Vol. 7, pp. 101-132. Austin: University of Texas Press.

Rodas, Flavio N., Ovidio C. Rodas, and Laurence F. Hawkins
1940   *Chichicastenango: The Kiche Indians, Their History and Culture: Sacred Symbols of Their Dress and Textiles*. Guatemala City: Sociedad de Geografia y Historia.

Sanders, William T.
1969   *The Pennsylvania State University Kaminaljuyu Project 1968 Season*. Department of Anthropology Occasional Papers in Anthropology, no. 2. University Park: Pennsylvania State University.

Siskin, Barbara
1977   "Changes in the Woven Design from Santo Tomas Chichicastenango." In *Ethnographic Textiles of the Western Hemisphere: Irene Emery Roundtable on Museum Textiles, 1976 Proceedings*, edited by Irene Emery and Patricia Fiske, pp. 154-156. Washington, D.C.: The Textile Museum.

Smith, Carol A.
1972   "The Domestic Marketing Systems of Western Guatemala." Unpublished Ph.D. dissertation, California: Stanford University.
1973   "The Evolution of Marketing Systems in Western Guatemala: A Central Place Analysis." *Estudios Sociales* 10:38-71.
1975   "Examining Stratification Systems Through Peasant Marketing Arrangements: An Application of Some Models from Economic Geography." *Man* 10,1:95-122.
1976   "Causes and Consequences of Central Place Types in Western Guatemala." In *Regional Analysis*, edited by Carol Smith, Vol. 1, pp. 255-299. New York: Academic Press.

Sperlich, Norman, and Elizabeth Katz Sperlich
1980   *Guatemalan Backstrap Weaving*. Norman: University of Oklahoma Press.

Start, Laura E.
1948   *The McDougall Collection of Indian Textiles from Guatemala and Mexico*. Pitt Rivers Museum, Occasional Papers on Technology, 2. Oxford: Oxford University Press.

Stout, Carol
1976   *Weavers of the Jade Needle: Textiles of Highland Guatemala*. Albuquerque: Maxwell Museum.

Tax, Sol
1963   *Penny Capitalism: A Guatemalan Indian Economy*. Chicago: University of Chicago Press.

Thompson, Sir J. Eric S.
1964   "Trade Relations Between the Maya Highlands and Lowlands." In *Estudios de Culture Maya*, Vol. 4. Mexico City: Centro de Estudios Mayas, Universidad Nacional.

Warren, Kay B.
1978   *The Symbolism of Subordination: Indian Identity in a Guatemalan Town*. Austin: University of Texas Press.

Wood, Josephine, and Lilly de Jongh Osborne
1966   *Indian Costumes of Guatemala*. Graz, Austria: Akademische Druck.

Woodward, Sue M.
1976   *Traditional Indian Costumes of Guatemala: Textiles from the Mathilda Geddings Gray Collection and Other Collections of the Middle American Research Institute*. New Orleans: Tulane University.